WIRTSCHAFTSWUNDER

Josef Heinrich Darchinger

WIRTSCHAFTS-WUNDER

Deutschland nach dem Krieg
Germany after the war

Klaus Honnef (Texte/text) – Frank Darchinger (Herausgeber/editor)

TASCHEN

Inhalt/Contents

Die fotografierte Zeit
Jupp Darchinger: Die 50er Jahre und die beginnenden 60er Jahre

Von Klaus Honnef

Je weiter der Blick in die Vergangenheit zurückgleitet, desto fantastischer erscheinen ihre fotografischen Darstellungen. Dabei haben die Bilder nach Ansicht vieler Theoretiker des Mediums doch konserviert, was tatsächlich einmal gewesen ist. Dennoch wirken Josef Heinrich Darchingers Aufnahmen aus den Anfängen der Bundesrepublik Deutschland, als hätte der Zauberer von Oz mit dem Schwung seines Stabes den Blick auf ein fremdes, merkwürdig unwirkliches Land ermöglicht. Die Menschen sind bescheiden und bieder gekleidet, Mädchen und Jungs schauen mit struppigen Haaren und munteren Gesichtern in die Kamera, die Auslagen der Geschäfte sind überschaubar, und die Autos haben den Charme von Oldtimern. Polizisten in Uniform regeln den spärlichen Verkehr an neuralgischen Punkten der Stadt unter einem metallenen Baldachin. Die städtische Architektur ist nüchtern und zweckmäßig, die Technik hingegen von handwerklichem Geist erfüllt. Durch das Land verläuft eine immer sichtbarer werdende Grenze aus spanischen Reitern, Stacheldraht und später Beton. Die Männer tragen alle Hut, und wo die Bomben des Krieges die Städte allgemeiner Vorstellung nach verwüstet hatten, stehen manchmal noch die unversehrten Bürgerhäuser der wilhelminischen Gründerjahre in stolzer Pracht. Verwundert reiben sich selbst diejenigen die Augen, die während der fotografierten Zeit aufgewachsen sind.

Umso fremder muss sie auf alle Menschen wirken, die geboren wurden, als viel breitere Straßen den Verkehr schon nicht mehr aufnehmen konnten und die Regale in den Warenhäusern von Angeboten überflossen, als Hüte aus der Mode gekommen waren und gelenkige Roboter in den Fertigungshallen der Autoindustrie die Arbeit erheblich schneller verrichteten als früher die Monteure mit ihren Händen am Fließband. Während die Welt der fotografischen Bilder ihren Großeltern im Blick zurück erscheint, als würden sie ihre Vergangenheit wie durch ein umgedrehtes Fernglas betrachten, nehmen die Jüngeren möglicherweise eher Züge des Exotischen wahr. Das äußere Erscheinungsbild des eigenen Landes während dieser Zeit ist ihnen vermutlich weniger vertraut als das ferner Länder in Amerika, Asien oder Afrika. Ein beziehungsreiches Echo auf die rheinischen Karnevalisten der unmittelbaren Nachkriegszeit, die nach dem Zusammenschluss der drei westlichen Besatzungszonen zu einer Wirtschaftseinheit selbstironisch schmetterten: „Wir sind die Eingeborenen von Trizonesien."

„Wenn nicht ein Wunder geschieht, geht das deutsche Volk zugrunde, langsam, aber sicher."

Was Darchingers Bilder im Spektrum von anderthalb Dekaden zeigen, konnten nicht einmal die Menschen damals, als er sie fotografierte, rational erklären.

Dabei haben sie die Zeit mit pragmatischem Elan und großer Energie bewältigt. Deshalb suchten sie in der Metaphysik Zuflucht und redeten von einem Wunder. Die Epoche, die der Fotograf porträtiert, ist als Zeit des „Wirtschaftswunders" im kollektiven Gedächtnis fest verankert. Auch Konrad Adenauer, der im September 1949 mit einer (seiner) Stimme Mehrheit zum ersten deutschen Bundeskanzler gewählt wurde, beschlich nach dem Ende des Zweiten Weltkrieges die vage Ahnung: „Wenn nicht ein Wunder geschieht, geht das deutsche Volk zugrunde, langsam, aber sicher." Keineswegs verwunderlich, wie ein paar trockene Zahlen und Statistiken belegen. 1,35 Millionen Tonnen Bomben waren auf die deutschen Städte gefallen, 3,6 Millionen Wohnungen wurden zerstört. Das Land, unter die vier Siegermächte USA, Großbritannien und Frankreich im Westen und die Sowjetunion im Osten aufgeteilt, lag politisch, wirtschaftlich, kulturell und moralisch am Boden. Die meisten seiner traditionsreichen Städte waren zu großen Teilen zerstört: Düren, Jülich, Wesel und Moers im Westen fast vollständig, Köln zu drei Vierteln, Hamburg zur Hälfte, Berlin, Dresden und München etwas weniger. Die alliierten Truppen hatten das Territorium vollständig besetzt und mit dem verbrecherischen Naziregime, dem die Deutschen in Scharen gefolgt waren, kurzen Prozess gemacht. Der deutsche Anteil am Blutzoll war hoch. Als Täter und als Opfer sind sie in der schrecklichen Bilanz aufgelistet. Zwar hatte man den Schutt beiseitegeräumt, minder beschädigte Häuser wieder hergerichtet und zahlreiche neue in blanker Funktionalität aufgebaut, doch die Ruinen gehörten ebenso zum geläufigen Erscheinungsbild wie die Kriegsversehrten, als Darchinger seine Laufbahn begann: ein Fotograf im Fachgebiet Journalismus. „Allen Gästen unserer Stadt – ein frohes Weihnachtsfest" wünscht in einem seiner frühen Bilder ein Transparent in Bonn, wo der Fotograf am 6. August 1925 geboren wurde. Aufgenommen am 25. Dezember 1952 in der Bahnhofstraße vor einem beschädigten Bürgerhaus der Gründerzeit mit einer Brandmauer, auf der wie auf einem Palimpsest die Konturen eines verschwundenen Nachbarhauses zu sehen sind. Der Krieg war überall gegenwärtig. Seit drei Jahren provisorische Hauptstadt der Bundesrepublik Deutschland, bot auch die Universitätsstadt Bonn, wiewohl vergleichsweise wenig zerstört, immerhin zu gut einem Drittel, einen grauen und eher trostlosen Anblick.

Darchinger gehört einer Generation an, die den Krieg trotz ihrer Jugend noch fast vollständig als aktiver Soldat, er als Panzersoldat, erlebte wie Helmut Schmidt, dessen politische Laufbahn er als Fotograf intensiv begleiten sollte. Nach Krieg und Kriegsgefangenschaft, aus der beim dritten Versuch die Flucht gelungen war, ließ Darchinger sich in Bonn zum Fotolaboranten ausbilden. Dass er dem Moloch Krieg entrann, schwer verwundet zwar, war für ihn das eigentliche Wunder. Den ursprünglich erlernten Beruf als Landwirt wollte er nie

Jupp Darchinger, der Fotograf, macht mit der Linhof Technika Aufnahmen vom Jochenstein-Stausee bei Passau. *1958*

Photographer Jupp Darchinger takes pictures of the Jochenstein reservoir near Passau with a Linhof Technika press camera. *1958*

Seite 6:
Mädchen lernen kochen — was denn sonst?, fragten damals fast alle. Auch in der Küche ist der Fortschritt unaufhaltsam. Haushaltsklasse in der Berufsschule Frankenberg in Hessen. *1956*

Page 6:
It goes without saying, in most people's opinions, that girls should be taught to cook. In the kitchen, too, progress is unstoppable. Domestic science class at the vocational school in Frankenberg, Hesse. *1956*

ergreifen, und mithilfe eines Programms für heimkehrende Soldaten, die ins zivile gesellschaftliche Gefüge wieder eingegliedert werden sollten, ließ er sich in einer „Umkehrentwicklungsanstalt" mit Namen Tempo GmbH zum Laboranten umschulen. Dort lernte er auch seine spätere Frau Ruth, eine ausgebildete Laborantin, kennen und lieben. Die Leiterin der Abteilung für Großfotografie wurde die unentbehrliche Partnerin seiner bald einsetzenden beruflichen Praxis – trotz ihrer zunehmenden familiären Verpflichtungen.

Die Firma Tempo GmbH war in der alten Bonner Fahnenfabrik untergebracht, deren Produkte vorübergehend nicht benötigt wurden. Einstige Direktoren der Agfa betrieben das Unternehmen. Weil sie intensiv in die Machenschaften der Nazidiktatur verstrickt gewesen waren, hatten sie vor den anrückenden Sowjets die Flucht ergriffen und sich mit Technikern, wertvollem Gerät und so viel Material, wie sie transportieren konnten, aus Wolfen im Osten nach Westen begeben, um eine neue Karriere zu beginnen. Etwa Bruno Uhl, der als Initiator der Weltmesse der Fotografie in Köln, der „Photokina", berühmt wurde. Die „Tempo GmbH" war lediglich eine Niederlassung. Doch für Darchinger sollte sie noch in anderer Weise wichtig werden. Denn als sich das Bedürfnis nach Farbbildern in der allmählich prosperierenden Bundesrepublik verstärkte, aktivierten die Agfa-Herren ihre nie abgerissenen Kontakte nach Wolfen, um Farbfilme zu importieren. Dort war man in der Lage, sie herzustellen, und im Westen hatte man die erforderlichen Farbchemikalien. Auch in der mitunter eisigen Luft des Kalten Krieges florierten solche Geschäfte auf Gegenseitigkeit. Darchinger gelangte dank seiner Beziehungen ohne besondere Schwierigkeiten in den Besitz von rarem Farbfilmmaterial für seine Arbeiten.

Als Fotograf tätig zu werden, ohne die vorgegebenen Stationen einer handwerklichen Laufbahn absolviert zu haben, war schwierig und forderte den hartnäckigen Widerstand der mächtigen Innung des Fotografenhandwerks heraus. Darum durfte sich Darchinger auch nicht als professioneller Fotograf beim Bonner Finanzamt anmelden. Als er stattdessen mit rheinischer Pfiffigkeit „Fotojournalist" vorschlug, legte sich die Behörde quer. Begründung: Der Beruf sei ihr nicht bekannt. Dass der Fotojournalismus 25 Jahre zuvor in Deutschland eine Blütezeit erlebt und kurz danach bei der Geburt der erfolgreichsten illustrierten Zeitschrift der westlichen Hemisphäre, bei „Life", Pate stand, hatte nicht zu seiner professionellen Anerkennung geführt. Gleichwohl gelang es Darchinger, den hinhaltenden Widerstand zu überwinden und sich als freier „Fotojournalist", der Erste unter diesem Label, zu etablieren.

Der Blick, den der Fotograf in den fünfziger und sechziger Jahren auf die Dinge warf, ist der eines genau und sorgfältig beobachtenden Zeitgenossen; sachlich und schnörkellos, auf das Entscheidende fixiert, formalen Spielereien abgeneigt.

Die wahrgenommene Szene optisch wirksam zu vermitteln war das Ziel. Das Bemühen um Sachlichkeit bedeutete keineswegs, auf eine eigene Haltung zu verzichten. Unverkennbar ablesbar ist das Interesse des Fotografen an sozialen „Missständen". Elend vergegenwärtigte er in ungeschöter Direktheit, beispielsweise die beklagenswerte Situation in den zahlreichen Flüchtlingslagern. Notunterkünfte nannte man sie – nicht um die Misere zu beschönigen, sondern um ihre Vorläufigkeit deutlich zu machen. Mitte der sechziger Jahre waren sie beseitigt. Darchinger thematisierte mit spürbarem Engagement das Schicksal der Rentner, die zu wenig zum Leben und zu viel zum Sterben hatten, der Kriegsversehrten, die zunächst kaum oder gar nicht vom Wirtschaftswunder profitierten, und der ein paar Jahre zuvor noch politisch Verfolgten. Schon früh klaffte die soziale Schere weit auseinander, und der Weg in die „Zweidrittelgesellschaft" war bereits hier vorgezeichnet. Bisweilen schimmert auch ein versteckter Hang zur Romantik in seinen Bildern durch, wenn er etwa einen kräftig dampfenden Schlepper im Rheingau vor erleuchtetem Himmel fotografierte, und durchgängig äußert sich ein leichtes Staunen angesichts der Dinge, die er aufzeichnete.

„Auf der Suche nach der verlorenen Zeit"

Das Staunen ist das vielleicht markanteste Merkmal in Darchingers Aufnahmen. Offenbar sah auch er sein Land mit den Augen eines Fremden an wie Andy Warhol später die USA. Gar nicht so fern der Wahrnehmung 60 oder 70 Jahre jüngerer Menschen; nur in umgekehrter Richtung. Denn seine prägenden Erfahrungen hatte Darchinger in der Nazizeit und in einem mörderischen Krieg mit anschließender Gefangenschaft gemacht. Eine völlig andere Welt. Was der Fotograf erblickte und mit seiner Kamera festhielt, war demzufolge Neuland für ihn, und mit dem Blick jenes Fremden, der in Marcel Prousts „Auf der Suche nach der verlorenen Zeit" nach langer Abwesenheit seine einstigen Freunde betrachtete, registrierte er den Umbruch, der sich vollzog, die Veränderungen, die den umfangreicheren Teil Deutschlands aus der Mitte Europas politisch und kulturell in den Westen katapultierten. Sah der Protagonist des französischen Schriftstellers nur die Spuren des Verfalls, erblickte Darchinger dagegen die Zeichen des Aufbruchs. Zugleich vergegenwärtigte er, bewusst und unbewusst, die offenen und latenten Widersprüche und Konflikte. Der Blick werde „immer schärfer, wenn die Umgebung nicht vertraut ist", bestätigte die Regisseurin Doris Dörrie. Darchinger hat sich diesen Blick bewahrt. Distanz, sagt der Fotograf, sei in seinem Beruf wesentlich. Es ist obendrein der Blick einer vorwiegend „skeptischen Generation". So hat der Soziologe Helmut Schelsky sie genannt. Nicht von der sprichwörtlichen Gedankenblässe angekränkelt, packte

Lebensmittelkarte der amerikanischen Besatzungszone. Die Lebensmittel waren knapp und deshalb strikt rationiert. Lebensmittelkarten regelten die Zuteilung. Ein Bezugsschein der amerikanischen Besatzungszone für Fleisch aus München. *1947*
Haus der Geschichte, Bonn

Ration card of the American zone of occupation. Food was in short supply and therefore strictly rationed. Ration cards regulated distribution. A coupon for meat, issued in the American zone of occupation, Munich. *1947*
Haus der Geschichte, Bonn

Fünf Millionen Pakete schickten private amerikanische Hilfsorganisationen unter dem Label CARE. Sie erschienen den meisten Deutschen wie ein Geschenk des Himmels, weil sie lang entbehrte Lebensmittel wie Dosenfleisch und Bohnenkaffee und manchmal auch Nylonstrümpfe enthielten. *1946–1948*
Haus der Geschichte, Bonn

Five million packages were sent by private American aid agencies under the CARE label. For most Germans, they were like a gift from heaven. Because they contained items they had gone without for years, such as tinned meat and real coffee, and sometimes even nylon stockings. *1946–1948*
Haus der Geschichte, Bonn

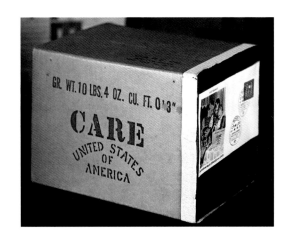

sie zu, orientierte sich am Möglichen, versuchte das Vergangene zu vergessen und im Streben nach materiellem Wohlstand eine Variante der „protestantischen Ethik" im Nachhall Max Webers zu leben. „Leistung wird den Nachkriegsdeutschen mit ihrem gebrochenen Nationalbewusstsein zum religiös aufgeladenen Ersatz für Volk und Vaterland", analysierte der Journalist und Historiker Klaus Wiegrefe. Pragmatismus prägte ihre Lebenshaltung. „Wir blickten nicht zurück", erinnerte sich Nicolaus Sombart. Verdrängung wird man den Menschen später ankreiden, obwohl das nur die halbe Wahrheit ist. Denn vom Krieg war häufig die Rede – in den illustrierten Zeitschriften, zu Hause, in Büchern und in den Kinos. Die Bilder Darchingers sind förmlich durchdrungen von einer Stimmung der Zuversicht, des Aufbruchs, des Lebenswillens, auch wenn die äußeren Umstände kläglich waren wie in den Baracken an der Peripherie der meisten Städte oder in den notdürftig hergerichteten Trümmerhäusern. Insgesamt zwölf Millionen Flüchtlinge waren aus den ehemaligen deutschen Ostgebieten und der Sowjetzone, der späteren DDR, in den Westen geströmt und mussten untergebracht werden, obwohl gerade im Westen Wohnraum äußerst knapp war. Auch wenn die Einheimischen sie mitunter abwehrend als „Polacken" beschimpften, ist es die vielleicht herausragendste Leistung der jungen bundesdeutschen Republik und ihrer Gesellschaft, dass die Integration der Flüchtlinge ziemlich reibungslos gelang. Der ökonomische Aufschwung im Kielwasser des Koreakrieges, der die Segel der Exportwirtschaft mächtig mit Wind füllte, förderte den Prozess, und der Fleiß und die Fertigkeiten der Vertriebenen verliehen ihm die notwendige Schubkraft.

Aus den Aufnahmen Darchingers spricht dennoch eine Sicht, die nicht ganz mit der übereinstimmt, die sich in der Erinnerung der nur anderthalb Jahrzehnte Jüngeren bewahrt hat – jener Generation der Kriegskinder, die den Bombenregen in den spärlich beleuchteten Luftschutzkellern durchzittert hatten, die in den gefährlich zerklüfteten und so verlockenden Trümmerlandschaften spielten und das Elend, den Mangel, die Kälte der Nachkriegszeit mit Schwarzmarkt, Hamsterfahrten aufs Land und grassierender Bandenkriminalität bewusst durchlebten. Wenn eine Bäckerei selten genug heiß begehrtes Weißbrot anpries, schickte die Mutter sie aus, und sie kehrten zu ihrem Ärger nach stundenlangem Ausharren in der Schlange mit dem klumpigen gelben Maisbrot zurück. Vielen waren die amerikanischen Soldaten wie Boten aus einem fernen, märchenhaften Land erschienen. Kaugummi, Schokolade, Dosenfleisch und die freundlichen GI Joes senkten eine tiefe Sehnsucht nach dem Land der scheinbar unbegrenzten Möglichkeiten und seiner Zivilisation in ihre Herzen. Sie waren am Ende der fünfziger Jahre die treibende Hefe, die den Laib der amerikanischen Populärkultur im Westen Deutschlands aufgehen ließ. In den Jahren ihres

Heranwachsens, dessen Folie Darchingers Aufnahmen abbilden, fühlten sie sich von den autoritären Strukturen einer auf das Bewährte fixierten Gesellschaft in ihrer Entwicklung gebremst. Die doppelte Moral der Einflussreichen und ihre bigotten Zensurbestrebungen stießen sie zusätzlich ab. Ihre Wahrnehmung mischt auch dunkle Schatten in die strahlenden Bilder des Wirtschaftswunders. In den Aufnahmen des Fotografen erkennen sie sich als fügsame Lehrlinge und adrett gekleidete Studenten beim Tanz, beim ungelenken Flirt oder als Mitglieder einer Musikband wieder. In der Tat war die Musik, genauer die amerikanische „Negermusik", wie konservative Kulturbeflissene abschätzig urteilten, ihr stärkster Ausdruck für den wachsenden Dissens. Jazz und vor allem Rock'n'Roll lieferten die Töne und die Rhythmen ihres nonverbalen Protestes.

Die meisten von ihnen standen bereits im Beruf, als die nachrückende Generation der 68er die Phase des Wiederaufbaus und die nach Adenauer benannte Epoche gründlich in Verruf brachte. Die 68er tauchten Darchingers Bilderwelt mit ihrer spezifischen Wahrnehmung in eine düstere Atmosphäre, eine, die sich der Veranschaulichung allerdings entzieht. Infolgedessen kreuzen sich in den Aufnahmen des Fotografen verschiedene Subtexte. Sie lassen sich je nach Perspektive und erfahrenem Leben mit unterschiedlichen Einsichten und Konsequenzen individuell entschlüsseln. Die Bilder sind zwar die gleichen geblieben. Doch ihre Interpretation verändert sich beständig.

Darchinger hat die Generation der nachmaligen 68er oft fotografiert, sozusagen *avant la lettre*. Nicht von ungefähr: Er war Familienvater. Die Jungs stolz mit ihren Rollern auf Ballonreifen und in kurzen Lederhosen. Wenn die pflegeleichten Beinkleider so speckig waren, dass sie nicht mehr zusammenfielen, wenn man sich ihrer entledigt hatte, waren sie richtig. Die Mädchen beim Spiel unter den Jungen oder beim Puppentheater. Wenn sie älter wurden, trennte man die Kinder in den staatlichen oder konfessionell gebundenen Schulen und in den Gymnasien nach Geschlechtern wie es die konservative Moral verlangte. Ein Paragraf im Gesetzbuch zieh selbst Eltern des strafwürdigen Vergehens der Kuppelei, wenn sie Jugendlichen unter 18 Jahren unter ihrem Dach eine gemeinsame Nacht gestatteten.

Bildung und Erziehung waren – und sind – Begriffe, die maßgebliche Politiker gerne im Munde führen. Auf der politischen Agenda stand schließlich das Problem eines fundamentalen Mentalitätswandels mit dem Ziel des mündigen Bürgers. Ein Mann wie der hessische Ministerpräsident Georg August Zinn demonstrierte sein Engagement auch persönlich, als er im Sommer 1956 eine der neuen Mittelpunktschulen besuchte. Auf den Bänken der Schule hatten wohl schon die Großväter der Schüler gesessen. Und in der Mehrzahl dienten als Lehrer dieselben, die während der braunen Zeit die nationalsozialistische

Plakat gegen den Schwarzmarkt-handel. Der Schwarzmarkt blühte. Das Geld war nichts wert. Besatzungsmächte und deutsche Stellen versuchten, ihn mit allen Mitteln einzudämmen. Razzien waren wirkungsvoller als Plakate, wenn auch nur vorübergehend. *1947*
Haus der Geschichte, Bonn

Poster against black-market trading. The black market flourished. Money was worth nothing. The occupying powers and German authorities did everything they could to contain it. Raids were more effective than posters, if only for a short time. *1947*
Haus der Geschichte, Bonn

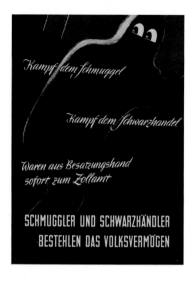

Ideologie vertreten hatten. Alternativen gab es kaum, solange die Nachfolger noch studierten. Nicht selten unterbrach in scheinbar unerwarteter Plötzlichkeit das absehbare Abitur in den Gymnasien den langsamen Fluss des chronologisch verabreichten Geschichtsunterrichts, sodass „Erster Weltkrieg" und „Zweiter Weltkrieg" in Kurzreferaten durchgepeitscht werden mussten, um den Lehrstoff ordnungsgemäß abzuschließen. Vom Völkermord kein Wort. Hat einer der korrekt frisierten Jungen von dem Bild mit dem hessischen Regierungschef zwölf Jahre später auf den Straßen Frankfurts und Berlins gegen die Staatsgewalt demonstriert, mit Pflastersteinen geworfen und über den minimalen Unterschied zwischen der Gewalt gegen Sachen und der Gewalt gegen Menschen gestritten? „Die Mehrheit der 68er hat … kein verrücktes Leben geführt", sagt der Schauspieler Elmar Wepper, einer von ihnen. Es sei das Mögliche, nicht das Wirkliche, das der Utopie den Platz versperre, schrieb Theodor W. Adorno einmal, einer der schärfsten und brillantesten Kritiker bürgerlich-kapitalistischer Gesellschaftsregime. Seine und die kritische Sicht der Frankfurter Schule prägten über Jahre das maßgebliche Bild der Wirtschaftswunderzeit.

Der aufmerksame Beobachter Darchinger hat den tragenden Säulen des Gesellschaftssystems der Bundesrepublik in seinen Bildern plastische Form gegeben: Politik, Industrie, Technik, Konsum und Bildung. Die Kultur im engeren Sinne fehlt, mit Ausnahme eines kabarettistischen Protestes gegen die deutsche Wiederbewaffnung, einen Preis, den Kanzler Adenauer für die – eingeschränkte – Souveränität des besiegten und besetzten Landes zu zahlen bereit war, gegen den Mehrheitswillen der Bevölkerung. Ursachen für das auffallende Defizit sind einerseits die Aufgaben, die der Fotograf in seinem Beruf je nach Anforderung zu bewältigen hatte. Im Auftrag der Sozialdemokratischen Partei war er oft unterwegs.

Er fertigte informative Tonbildschauen zur Unterrichtung und Porträts der Parteigrößen für Wahlkämpfe an, Aufträge, die ihm Zutritt zum Kreis der Politiker verschafften. Darüber hinaus produzierte er Postkarten und realisierte Aufnahmen für alle möglichen Zeitungen und illustrierte Blätter. Andererseits war der ungeheure kulturelle Nachholbedarf der unmittelbaren Nachkriegszeit verflogen, als der Fotograf seine absichtslose Chronik begann, und materielle Interessen hatten die kulturellen abgelöst. Das Kino florierte wie noch nie und signalisierte ein wachsendes Unterhaltungsbedürfnis. Allein vier Filme neben einer Kunstausstellung, einem Tanzkurs, einer politischen Veranstaltung und einem „Box-Großkampftag" mit dem populären Peter Müller oder „Müllers Aap", wie der Volksmund den Mittelgewichtler seines verwegenen Gesichts wegen taufte, kündigte eine Kölner Plakatwand im Juni 1956 an. Das Fernsehen eroberte die Wohnzimmer und verdrängte das Radio aus dem Mittelpunkt der

Aufmerksamkeit. Es wird nicht nur das Universum der Bilder, sondern kraft seiner Bilder auch die Welt und das Verhalten der Menschen substanziell verändern. Ein Prozess, den Darchingers politische Fotos für das Magazin „Der Spiegel" (intensiver seit 1964) und die Wochenzeitung „Die Zeit" einprägsam dokumentieren.

Die Arbeiter waren das Fundament des wirtschaftlichen Aufschwungs

Die intellektuellen Kreise empfanden sich in den fünfziger Jahren überwiegend als Hort der Opposition gegen die vorherrschenden Verhältnisse im Land. Die regierende CDU und ihre Satelliten galten vielen als zu reaktionär, die oppositionelle SPD als zu spießig. Im Gegenzug beschimpften die Politiker der Regierung die aufmüpfigen Kulturgrößen manchmal als „Ratten" oder „Schmeißfliegen". Erst mit dem Auftreten von Willy Brandt wandelten sich die Beziehungen grundlegend. Darchinger fotografierte 1965 den charismatischen Regierenden Bürgermeister von Berlin und seit Kurzem Chef der größten Oppositionspartei auf einer Wahlkampftour bei einer eigens organisierten Veranstaltung in Bayreuth, als er dem dozierenden Schriftsteller Günter Grass und anderen Intellektuellen zuhörte.

Umso beeindruckender rückte der Fotograf die Menschen ins Bild, die den wirtschaftlichen Aufschwung der jungen Bundesrepublik Deutschland antrieben, und versah sie mit unverwechselbaren Gesichtern. Die Stahlarbeiter einer Eisengießerei, die männlichen und weiblichen Monteure in der Elektroindustrie, die Drucker an der Rotation eines Zeitungsverlages, die Straßenarbeiter, die dem Land trotz ihrer altertümlichen Teerkocher die notwendige Infrastruktur schufen, die Kumpel unter Tage, die über Tage gegen die Schließung ihrer unrentablen Zechen demonstrierten, die Werft- und Hafenarbeiter in den Küstenstädten, die Kundenbetreuerinnen im Versandhaus – die Schlote rauchen wieder, hieß es, und fast alle registrierten das mit Genugtuung. Manche Bilder erinnern an Fernsehfilme, die zwanzig Jahre später gedreht wurden, andere atmen den Geist, der populäre zeitgenössische Science-Fiction-Serien beeinflusste. Die Fiktion hat sie im Nachhinein und ohne ihr Dazutun unter ihr Regime gezwungen.
Arbeit am Samstag war selbstverständlich, Arbeitsschutz wurde kleingeschrieben. Die Entschlossenheit, den sprichwörtlichen Karren aus dem Dreck zu ziehen, verband, und der sich verhältnismäßig rasch abzeichnende wirtschaftliche Erfolg versöhnte mit dem ungewohnten demokratischen Regiment. Nicht wenige teilten ursprünglich die Meinung des Nobelpreisträgers Thomas Mann, die der Schriftsteller lange vor seinem Kampf gegen die Naziherrschaft aus dem

In Nürnberg fanden die ersten Prozesse in der Geschichte gegen Kriegsverbrecher statt. Angeklagt waren die überlebenden politischen und militärischen Spitzen Nazideutschlands. Die Prozesse waren unpopulär. Plakate begründeten ihre Motive. *1945/1946*
Haus der Geschichte, Bonn

The first trials in history against war criminals took place in Nuremberg. In the dock were the surviving members of Nazi Germany's political and military élite. The trials were unpopular. Posters explained their motives. *1945/1946*
Haus der Geschichte, Bonn

Der erste deutsche Nachkriegsfilm „Die Mörder sind unter uns" (1946) von Wolfgang Staudte rechnete mit den Verbrechen der Vergangenheit in eindrucksvollen Bildern ab. Doch er betonte zu stark die Ohnmacht des Einzelnen angesichts schwerer Herausforderungen.
Haus der Geschichte, Bonn

The first German postwar film "The Murderers Are Among Us" (1946) by Wolfgang Staudte settled the score with the crimes of the past in powerful images. But it placed too much emphasis on the powerlessness of the individual in the face of difficult challenges.
Haus der Geschichte, Bonn

kalifornischen Exil in den seinerzeit viel zitierten „Betrachtungen eines Unpolitischen" (1918) geäußert hatte: der „vielverschriene ‚Obrigkeitsstaat' [sei] die dem deutschen Volk angemessene, zukömmliche und von ihm im Grunde gewollte Staatsform" und bleibe es. Die autoritäre Führung der Regierungsgeschäfte durch Adenauer schien die Ansicht des Autors zu bestätigen, zumal sie äußerst erfolgreich war. Und sie ermöglichte auch denjenigen Menschen einen stillschweigenden Wechsel ihrer Haltung, die nicht als lupenreine Demokraten das Licht der Welt erblickt hatten.

Wer jedoch genauer hinschaut, erkennt in Darchingers Bildern unter der optimistischen Oberfläche eine Wirklichkeit der tiefen Widersprüche. Impulse entschlossener Modernisierung und zähes Festhalten am Althergebrachten überlagerten sich. Nicht einmal die Verwendung der Farbe verbirgt die scharfen Bruchlinien. Einer wachsenden Automatisierung in Industrie und Landwirtschaft, dem technischen Fortschritt in der Medizin, einer rapiden Rationalisierung in der Bürokratie begegneten erstarrte Rituale aus längst vergangenen Zeiten im öffentlichen Leben, privater Biedersinn mit abendlicher Versammlung der Familie vor dem neuen Hausaltar, dem Fernsehen, und das streng hierarchische Gefüge in den privaten und öffentlichen Einrichtungen wie Familie, Schule, Universität, Verwaltung und Politik.

Die Frauen mussten ihren Mann um Erlaubnis fragen, wenn sie einen Beruf ergreifen wollten

Signifikant ist in diesem Zusammenhang die Rolle der Frauen in den ersten Jahren der Bundesrepublik. Junge Frauen, gern als „Mädchen" apostrophiert, lernten in den Haushaltsklassen der Berufsschulen kochen, um einen Haushalt mit Mann und Kindern führen zu können, andere immerhin das Frisörhandwerk. In der Landwirtschaft mussten alle, unbeschadet ihres Alters, bei Aussaat und Ernte anpacken. Nach der Währungsreform 1948 waren die Frauen, die während des Krieges die Männer in den Fabriken und Büros ersetzt hatten, in die Küche zurückbeordert worden. Doch die wirtschaftliche Prosperität mit durchschnittlichen Wachstumsraten von 8,5 % führte rasch zu einem akuten Mangel an geeigneten Arbeitskräften. Dies bahnte den Frauen erneut den Zugang zu einer beruflichen Tätigkeit jenseits des vom deutschen Film und den Zeitschriften propagierten Hausfrauendaseins im Ehegespann. Und diese versprach obendrein finanzielle Unabhängigkeit. Um 1955 stellten die Frauen bereits ein Drittel sämtlicher in einem Beruf Beschäftigten. Die verheirateten benötigten noch die Erlaubnis ihrer Ehemänner. Ein weiterer eklatanter Widerspruch der Zeit: Konten unterhalten durften Frauen ebenfalls nicht;

es sei denn, mit dem Plazet des Gatten, wobei dieser die Zinsen kassieren durfte. Die Dissonanzen klangen nur unterschwellig an. Sie manifestierten sich in Nuancen. Dem aufmerksamen Beobachter Darchinger entgingen sie gleichwohl nicht. Als die berüchtigte Fresswelle anrollte, kündeten die penibel in Reih und Glied aufgestapelten Konserven der sogenannten Feinkostgeschäfte von einem sich verstärkenden Wohlstand zehn Jahre nach der bedingungslosen Kapitulation Nazideutschlands. Die Schaufenster waren prall gefüllt und sonnten sich im Überfluss der Waren. Dosenkost war unter den Besserverdienenden der „letzte Schrei"; der obligate Hummercocktail mit den Stücken des Schalentieres aus der Konserve dokumentierte das gehobene soziale Prestige des jeweiligen Gastgebers. Außerdem lieferten die Konserven ein untrügliches Indiz für den Wandel des Ernährungsstils in der Spätmoderne und einen Hinweis auf die langsame Befreiung der Frauen aus der überkommenen Küchenfron. Aus der Dose in den Topf und auf den Tisch, lautete die Devise in einer steigenden Anzahl von Familien. Langwierige Vorbereitungen entfielen, und umfangreiche Vorratswirtschaft war mit Konserven auch kein Problem. Frische Lebensmittel halten sich bekanntlich nur einige Tage, und Kühlschränke, die nachhaltiger als sämtliche übrigen technischen Errungenschaften den Alltag und die Lebensgewohnheiten umkrempelten, weil sie langfristige Bevorratung erlauben, besaßen erst die wenigsten Haushalte. Vor dem Hintergrund der bunten Dosenkultur in den Feinkostläden entbrannte anlässlich der saisonalen Ausverkäufe in den Warenhäusern der Stadtzentren, die den traditionellen Einzelhandel mit persönlichem Kundenkontakt in die Außenbezirke verbannt hatten, eine Schlacht um Sonderangebote und die billigste Kleidung. Nicht bloß die Schattenmenschen des Wirtschaftswunders stürzten sich ins Getümmel um die „Schnäppchen". Die Amerikanisierung der Bundesrepublik setzte sich unmerklich, aber unaufhaltsam fort. Im Konsumverhalten realisierte sie sich zuerst. Darchinger markierte gelegentlich ihre sichtbaren Signale an den Brennpunkten des Interesses, am Potsdamer Platz in Berlin direkt an der Demarkationslinie das Markenzeichen der weltweit operierenden Firma Coca-Cola oder in der Mensa der Hochschulen die charakteristischen Flaschen der Limonadenfabrik, deren Produkt das bevorzugte Getränk der Studenten wurde. Auch die Lichter der Großstädte, die seine Aufnahmen wiedergeben, ahmten amerikanische Vorbilder nach. Hollywood verdrängte den deutschen Film aus den deutschen Kinos und expandierte, bis es die bundesrepublikanischen Leinwände nahezu unumschränkt beherrschte. Und Comics, von den Lehrern als sittenverderbendes Teufelszeug angeprangert, fanden im Lande Wilhelm Buschs ihre Fans und wurden nicht nur unter den Schulbänken gelesen. Auch die amerikanische Literatur erreichte in deutschen Übersetzungen hohe Auflagen: Ernest Hemingway, William Faulkner, John Dos

Die SED rief in der sowjetischen Besatzungszone dazu auf, den Halbjahresplan 1948 ohne Hilfe des Marshall-Planes zu erfüllen. „Hinaus! Wir brauchen keinen Marshall-Plan, wir kurbeln selbst die Wirtschaft an!"
Nordrhein-Westfälisches Staatsarchiv, Detmold

In the Soviet-occupied zone, the SED called for the half-year plan for 1948 to be implemented without help from the Marshall Plan. "Out! We need no Marshall Plan, we can reflate the economy ourselves!"
Nordrhein-Westfälisches Staatsarchiv, Detmold

„Wir werden besser leben." Obwohl die Frauen den Männern gesetzlich gleichgestellt werden, glauben Tausende nicht an die strahlende Zukunft der stalinistischen Propaganda und verlassen die DDR über die noch relativ durchlässige Grenze in Richtung Westen. Das Plakat zum Fünfjahresplan 1951 der DDR lacht über die traurige Realität hinweg.
Haus der Geschichte, Bonn

"Life will be better for us". Although women have equality with men by law, thousands have no faith in the glowing future of Stalinist propaganda and leave the GDR by the still relatively open border to the West. The poster promoting the GDR's 1951 five-year plan puts a smiling face on the sad reality.
Haus der Geschichte, Bonn

Passos und Thornton Wilder für die Kulturbewussten, Dashiell Hammett, Raymond Chandler, Ross Macdonald und Mickey Spillane für die Krimiliebhaber. Mit seinen erschwinglichen Taschenbüchern war der Rowohlt Verlag ein wichtiger Transmissionsriemen. Drei der vier Krimiautoren werden inzwischen auch in Deutschland als Literaten von Format begriffen.

Für die jungen Deutschen verkörperte Kennedy die Hoffnung auf Veränderung

Die Jahre der Nachkriegszeit und des Wirtschaftswunders neigten sich ihrem Ende zu, als der blutjunge Senator John F. Kennedy den Vizepräsidenten der verknöcherten Regierung des Weltkriegsgenerals Eisenhower und zutiefst unsympathischen Richard „Tricky Dicky" Nixon im amerikanischen Wahlkampf herausforderte. Der Generation der Kriegskinder in der westlichen Welt erschien er wie die leibhaftige Verkörperung der tief ersehnten Veränderung; als die Verheißung eines prinzipiellen Kurswechsels der westlichen Politik und als der Befreier aus dem verkrusteten Moralkorsett der Nachkriegszeit. Im Juni 1963, zwei Jahre nachdem die Machthaber in der DDR den Osten Deutschlands mit einer Mauer eingeschlossen hatten, besuchte er als Präsident der USA die Bundesrepublik. Darchinger fotografierte Kennedy, lässig und sorglos von seinen Bodyguards bewacht, bei der Ankunft. Kein *Cordon sanitaire*, der die Politprominenz ein knappes halbes Jahrhundert nach seinem Besuch vor den Menschen abschirmen wird. Im eingeschlossenen Westberlin flogen dem amerikanischen Präsidenten die Herzen der Berliner zu, als er verkündete: „Ich bin ein Berliner." Niemand ahnte, dass er ein schwer kranker Mann und eine wandelnde Apotheke war. Wenige Monate später wurde er ermordet. Kennedy, der den Sieg im amerikanischen Wahlkampf seiner erfrischenden Jugendlichkeit, einer schönen und glamourösen Frau an seiner Seite und der besseren Figur im Fernsehen im Vergleich zu seinem Rivalen verdankte, hat die Spielregeln der Politik trotz seiner kurzen Amtszeit vollständig neu gestaltet.
Die unverhohlenen Sympathien der jungen Deutschen für Kennedy übertrugen sich auf Willy Brandt. Er war bald der Kanzlerkandidat der SPD und warf, wenn auch zunächst vergeblich, gegen den CDU-Patriarchen Konrad Adenauer seinen Hut in den Ring. Darchinger hat zahlreiche seiner Wahlreisen als Fotograf begleitet: die Fahrten im offenen Wagen mit neugierigen Kindern statt misstrauischen Personenschützern im Schlepptau und die umjubelten Auftritte in der überfüllten Dortmunder Westfalenhalle. Fernsehpräsenz und telegene Wirkung gaben zu jener Zeit noch nicht den Ausschlag bei der Wahlentscheidung.

Der schlimmste Makel der westdeutschen Erfolgsstory von Wiederaufbau, wirtschaftlichem Aufschwung und internationaler Anerkennung entzieht sich fotografischer Evidenz. Kaum hatte die Bundesrepublik ihre Souveränität zumindest im Inneren erreicht, erlahmten die Anstrengungen, überlebende Täter des „Dritten Reiches" vor Gericht zu stellen und einer gerechten Strafe zuzuführen. Ihre unvorstellbaren Verbrechen verloren sich außer Sichtweite. Die bunten Farben des Wirtschaftswunders übertünchten das Grauen der Vergangenheit. Nationalsozialismus und „totaler Krieg" mutierten im öffentlichen Bewusstsein zu unbegreiflichen Schicksalsschlägen. Vielen der maßgeblich Beteiligten gelang die Flucht ins Ausland. Eine größere Menge nistete sich in den staatlichen und privatwirtschaftlichen Institutionen der jungen Bundesrepublik ein. Einer der offiziellen Kommentatoren der berüchtigten Nürnberger Rassengesetze avancierte sogar zum Chef des Bundeskanzleramtes und saß sämtliche Vorwürfe bis zu seiner Pensionierung aus. Aber nicht nur die Schreibtischtäter setzten ihre frühere Arbeit in Verwaltung, Justiz, Medizin, Polizei, Medien und Hochschule ungehindert fort, manche Schergen ebenfalls. „Wir haben nichts gewusst", ließen die tief Verstrickten unisono verlautbaren, als die Generation der 68er ihre bohrenden Fragen stellte. Nichts haben sie gewusst von den Konzentrationslagern und dem planmäßig betriebenen Vernichtungskrieg im Osten. Als wären ihre Mitbürger im Naziland nicht mit gelben Sternen öffentlich gebrandmarkt, aus ihren Häusern vertrieben und am Ende in die Viehwagen der Eisenbahn gepfercht worden; als wären die endlosen Waggons nicht über die Schienen „des Reiches" gerollt und stunden- oder auch tagelang auf offener Strecke oder in den Güterbahnhöfen abgestellt worden, um „kriegswichtige" Züge passieren zu lassen. Und die heimkehrenden Soldaten, die von den Massakern wussten, schwiegen wie die Daheimgebliebenen. Vor diesem Ausblenden der Verantwortung für die eigene Geschichte muss die sonst so genaue Fotografie Josef Heinrich Darchingers kapitulieren.

Von Jahr zu Jahr wird der Straßenverkehr dichter auf dem Marienplatz am Münchner Rathaus. *1963*

Year by year, the traffic on the Marienplatz in front of Munich's town hall gets busier. *1963*

A Time Photographed
Jupp Darchinger: The Fifties and early Sixties

By Klaus Honnef

The further time recedes into the past, the more bizarre its photographic images appear to be. Yet according to many theorists of the medium, it is such images that preserve the true reality of how things actually were. Nevertheless, Josef H. Darchinger's photographs from the early years of the Federal Republic of Germany somehow make us feel that the Wizard of Oz has waved his magic wand and allowed us to look into a strange and oddly unreal world. The clothes people wear are homely and sedate, girls and boys stare into the camera with cheerful faces and unkempt hair, the goods in the shops are limited in range and the cars are all classics. Policemen in uniform direct the sparse traffic at critical points in the town under a metal canopy. City architecture is plain and functional; technology, on the other hand, is still harnessed to the craftsman's trade. An increasingly visible dividing line runs through the country, built of barbed-wire barriers, razor wire and then concrete. All the men wear hats, and where the war-time bombing was generally thought to have laid the cities waste, the unscathed town houses of the Wilhelminian period of industrial expansion occasionally still stand in all their splendour. Even people who grew up in the time photographed can hardly believe their eyes.

It must seem even stranger to all those people who were born when much wider roads were already failing to cope with the traffic, and the shelves in the department stores overflowed with a superfluity of goods; when hats were out of fashion and in the production sheds of the automotive industry, nimble robots performed the tasks very much faster than the mechanics had once done manually on the assembly line. While the world of the photographic images makes their grandparents feel in retrospect that they are seeing their own past through the wrong end of a telescope, the impression of the younger generation is more likely to be of something rather exotic. The external image of their native country during this period is probably less familiar to them than that of faraway lands in the Americas, Asia or Africa. There are rich associations here with the carnivalists in the Rhineland immediately after the war, whose response to the formation of an economic union by the three Western zones of occupation was a song belted out with ironic gusto: "We are the natives of Trizonesia…"

"Without a miracle, the German nation will slowly but surely go to rack and ruin."

What Darchinger's photographs show across the spectrum of one and a half decades, is something not even the people then, at the time when he was taking their pictures, could provide a rational explanation for. Yet they were the ones who made it happen, with pragmatic élan and enormous energy. That is why

they resorted to metaphysics and spoke in terms of a miracle. The years the photographer portrays are anchored firmly in the collective memory as years of an economic miracle. Even Konrad Adenauer, who was elected the first Federal Chancellor in September 1949 with a majority of one vote, his own, was beset after the end of the Second World War by the vague presentiment: "Without a miracle, the German nation will slowly but surely go to rack and ruin." Not at all surprising, as a few plain figures and details will make clear. 1.35 million tonnes of bombs had been dropped on German cities, 3.6 million homes were destroyed. The country, partitioned among the four victorious powers – the USA, Great Britain and France in the West and the Soviet Union in the East – was politically, economically, culturally and morally on its knees. Most of its tradition-steeped cities were largely in ruins. Düren, Jülich, Wesel and Moers in the West were totally destroyed, as were three-quarters of Cologne, half of Hamburg, and to a somewhat lesser extent Berlin, Dresden and Munich. The Allied troops had occupied the whole of the territory and dealt summarily with the criminal Nazi regime, which the Germans had followed in droves. The German share in the death toll was high. They are listed on the horrifying balance sheet, both as perpetrators and as victims.

The rubble had been cleared away, less damaged houses patched up and countless new ones built in faceless functionality. But the ruins and the disabled ex-servicemen were part of the familiar scene when Darchinger started out on his career as a photographer in the field of journalism. "A Merry Christmas to everyone visiting our town" proclaims a banner in one of his early pictures. The town is Bonn, where the photographer was born on 6 August 1925. Taken on 25 December 1952 near the station in Bahnhofstraße in front of a bomb-damaged Wilhelminian town house with a party wall on which, like a palimpsest, the contours of what was once the neighbouring house can be traced. The war made its presence felt everywhere. Chosen as the provisional federal capital three years earlier, the university town of Bonn, with comparatively little, though still a third of its substance damaged, presented a grey and rather cheerless appearance. Like Helmut Schmidt, whose political career he would later follow, Darchinger, who was with the tank corps, belongs to a generation which, despite their youth, saw active military service virtually throughout the war. After war service and captivity as a prisoner of war, from which he managed to escape at the third attempt, Darchinger had qualified as a photo lab technician in Bonn. For him, escaping from the juggernaut of war, badly wounded though he was, was the real miracle. As he had never wanted to work as a farmer, this being the career he had originally trained for, he enrolled in a programme for the social integration of soldiers returning from the war and retrained as a laboratory technician in a

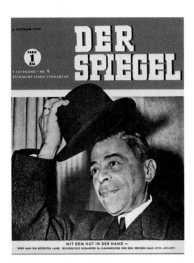

In Hannover erschien die erste Ausgabe des Wochenblattes „Der Spiegel". Die britische Besatzungsmacht erteilte die Erlaubnis. Rudolf Augstein hieß der Herausgeber. „Der Spiegel" stieg binnen kurzer Zeit zur politisch einflussreichsten Zeitschrift im Westen Deutschlands auf. *4. Januar 1947*
Spiegel-Verlag, Hamburg

The first edition of the weekly magazine *Der Spiegel* **appeared in Hanover,** with the permission of the British occupying power. The publisher was Rudolf Augstein. Within a short time, *Der Spiegel* rose to become the most politically influential magazine in the west of Germany.
4 January 1947
Spiegel Verlag, Hamburg

Seite 14:
Attraktion. Der Blick über die Mauer ist für Politiker auf ihren Reisen nach Westberlin Besucherpflicht und für die Touristen ein Spektakel. Was früher erschütterte, verkommt zum allfälligen Ritual. Man gewöhnt sich auch an das Ungewöhnliche. *1962*

Page 14:
Attraction. A look over the Wall is an absolute must for politicians visiting West Berlin and a spectacle for the tourists. What shook people to the core at first is degenerating into something of a ritual. People get used to the unusual. *1962*

reversal processing firm called Tempo GmbH. There he also met and fell in love with his wife Ruth, a qualified lab technician, head of the department of macrophotography and indispensable partner – despite her increasing family responsibilities – in what would soon become his professional practice.

Tempo GmbH was housed in the old flag factory in Bonn, whose products were temporarily not required. The company was run by former directors of Agfa. Because of their deep involvement in the machinations of the Nazi dicatorship, they had opted for flight before the Soviet advance and had left Wolfen in the East, with technicians, valuable equipment and as much material as they could carry and come to the West to start a new career. Dr. Bruno Uhl, for example, who achieved fame as the initiator of the World Photography Fair in Cologne, otherwise known as "Photokina". Tempo GmbH was just a subsidiary. But it would become important for Darchinger in another way. Because as the demand for colour photographs increased in the gradually prospering Federal Republic, the Agfa people reactivated their contacts with Wolfen, which had never been broken off, in order to import colour films. They were able to produce them there, and the West had the necessary colour chemicals. Even in the sometimes glacial atmosphere of the cold war, the business flourished reciprocally. Thanks to his connections, Darchinger was able to obtain rare film material for his projects without too much difficulty.

To work as a photographer without having completed the stages prescribed for training in a skilled trade was problematic and provoked stubborn opposition from the powerful craftsmen's guild of photographers. For this reason, too, Darchinger was not allowed to register with the tax office in Bonn as a professional photographer. With Rhenish quick thinking, he then suggested "photojournalist" as an alternative, but the authorities turned this down flat on the grounds that the profession was not known to them. The fact that photojournalism had had its heyday 25 years earlier in Germany and had shortly afterwards been the force behind the launch of *Life*, the most successful illustrated magazine in the western hemisphere, had not led to the profession being given an official seal. Nevertheless, Darchinger succeeded in overcoming the persistent opposition and establishing himself as a freelance "photojournalist", the first under that label.

The eye the photographer cast on things in the Fifties and Sixties is that of a meticulous and scrupulous contemporary observer, dispassionate and unequivocal. Focusing on the crucial point, loath to play formal games. The aim was to convey with visual impact what he had seen. His concern for objectivity in no way meant foregoing a personal standpoint. The photographer's interest in social injustice is unmistakable. He gave destitution a visible face with stark immediacy,

as he found it in the lamentable conditions of the countless refugee camps. Emergency shelters, they were called, not to gloss over the wretchedness but to emphasize their provisional nature. They were cleared in the mid-Sixties. With palpable commitment, Darchinger made a central theme of the lot of the pensioners with too little to live and too much to die, the disabled ex-servicemen, who at first benefited little or not at all from the economic miracle, and those who just a few years earlier had been the victims of political persecution. The social divide opened wide at an early stage, and the road was paved to the "two-thirds society". Occasionally, too, a hidden vein of romanticism shines through in his pictures, for instance in his shot of a tug in the Rheingau belching out steam against the golden glow of the sky, and there is throughout a sense of mild astonishment in the face of the things he recorded.

"In Search of Lost Time"

The astonishment is perhaps the most striking feature in Darchinger's photographs. Clearly, he looked at his own country with the eyes of a stranger, as Andy Warhol later looked at the USA. Not so far removed from the perceptions of people sixty or seventy years younger, only in the opposite direction. Because Darchinger's formative experiences had been gathered in the Nazi period and in a murderous war followed by captivity. A totally different world. Accordingly, what the photographer saw and recorded with his camera was virgin land for him, and with the eye of the stranger in Marcel Proust's "In Search of Lost Time", contemplating his old friends after a long absence, he registered the transformation that was taking place, the changes that were catapulting the larger part of Germany politically and culturally out of the centre of Europe and into the West. If the French writer's observer saw only the signs of decay, Darchinger in contrast saw the signs of a new awakening. At the same time, he made manifest, consciously and unconsciously, the obvious and the latent contradictions and conflicts. The eye gets "sharper and sharper when the surroundings are unfamiliar", affirmed the film director Doris Dörrie. Darchinger has kept this sharp eye. Distance, the photographer says, is essential in his profession.

It is, furthermore, the eye of a largely "sceptical generation", as sociologist Helmut Schelsky has called them. Not "sicklied o'er with the pale cast of thought", they act with resolution, go for what is possible, try to forget the past and seek in the pursuit of material prosperity to live out a variant of the "protestant ethic" echoing Max Weber. "For the postwar Germans with their fractured national consciousness", thus goes the analysis of journalist and historian Klaus

Am 24. Juni 1952 kam im Verlag Axel Springer die erste Ausgabe der „Bild-Zeitung" heraus. Rasch überflügelte das marktschreierische Boulevardblatt in punkto Auflage alle anderen deutschen Zeitungen.
Haus der Geschichte, Bonn

On 24 June 1952, the first edition of the *Bild-Zeitung* was released by the Axel Springer Publishing House. The strident tabloid rapidly overtook all the German newspapers in terms of circulation.
Haus der Geschichte, Bonn

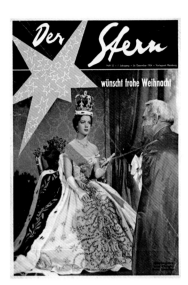

Das Cover der Illustrierten „Der Stern" vom 26. Dezember 1954 zeigt die blutjunge Romy Schneider als britische Königin Victoria. Zwei Jahre später wird die Schauspielerin die Herzen des Kinopublikums als Kaiserin „Sissi" im Sturm erobern.
Haus der Geschichte, Bonn

The cover of the illustrated magazine *Der Stern* of 26 December 1954 shows the very young Romy Schneider as Britain's Queen Victoria. Two years later, the actress will take the hearts of the cinema-going public by storm in her role as Empress "Sissi".
Haus der Geschichte, Bonn

Wiegrefe, "efficiency is the religiously charged substitute for nation and fatherland." Pragmatism shaped their attitude to life. "We didn't look back", Nicolaus Sombart remembers. Later they would be accused of not facing up to the facts, although that is only half the truth. Because war often was the subject, in the illustrated magazines, at home, in books and in the cinemas. Darchinger's pictures are literally steeped in a mood of confidence, of a new start, of the will to live. Even when the outward circumstances were deplorable, as in the hut camps on the periphery of most cities or in the roughly patched-up, bomb-damaged houses. A total of 12 million refugees had streamed across to the West from the former eastern territories of Germany and the Soviet zone, the later GDR, and had to be integrated, although there was a huge housing shortage, particularly in the west of the country. And if the locals, who were also suffering from the scarcity of housing, occasionally berated them as "Polacks", it is still perhaps the most outstanding achievement of the Federal German Republic and its society that the integration of the refugees was accomplished relatively smoothly. The economic upturn in the wake of the Korean War, which fuelled a huge boom in exports, benefited the process, and the hard work and skills of the expellees lent it the necessary thrust.

What comes across from Darchinger's photographs, however, is a view of things that does not quite correspond with the one lodged in the memories of those who were just a decade and a half younger. Of the generation of war children. They had shaken with fear under the rain of bombs in the dimly-lit air-raid shelters, they played in the dangerously riven and irresistibly inviting landscapes of the bomb sites, and had undergone in full awareness the hardship, the deprivation, the cold of the postwar period with the black market, the foraging trips to the countryside and mounting gang crime. When a bakery, rarely enough, advertised a batch of highly sought-after white bread, their mother would send them for it, and they would return, to their chagrin, after hours of queueing, with the lumpy yellow corn bread. To many of them, the American soldiers seemed like messengers from a distant fairytale country. Chewing gum, chocolate, tins of spam and the friendly GIs planted in their hearts a deep longing for the land of apparently unlimited possibilities and its civilization. At the end of the Fifties, they were the leaven that caused the dough of American popular culture to rise in the west of Germany. In the years when they were growing up, against the background depicted in Darchinger's photographs, they felt continually restricted in their development by the authoritarian structures of a society fixated on the tried and tested. The double standards of the people with influence and their bigoted efforts to censor everything alienated them further. Their perceptions introduce dark shadows into the vibrant images of the eco-

nomic miracle. They recognize themselves in Darchinger's photographs as biddable apprentices and smartly dressed students at a dance, making a clumsy attempt to flirt or playing in a band. It was the music, or more precisely the American "negro music", as conservative cultural snobs disparagingly called it, that was the strongest expression of their gradually mounting dissent. Jazz and especially rock'n'roll supplied the sounds and the rhythms of their non-verbal protest.

Most of them were already in employment when the next generation, the "68ers", cast a well and truly dubious light on the phase of reconstruction and the so-called Adenauer era. The 68ers caused Darchinger's world of images, with its particular account of things, to be seen as veiled in a sinister atmosphere, albeit one that resists apprehension. As a result, different subtexts run counter to each other in the photographer's pictures. They are decoded with different insights and consequences according to the standpoint and life experience of each individual. The images remain the same. But the way they are interpreted changes all the time.

Darchinger often photographed the generation of future 68ers, avant la lettre, as it were. Not by chance: he was a father himself. The boys confidently handling their scooters with the balloon tyres, and dressed in leather shorts. When these low-maintenance breeches were so greasy that they stood up on their own when you took them off, they were just right. The girls playing together with the boys or watching a puppet show. When they got older, division according to gender was gaining ground in the state or faith schools and in the grammar schools. Conservative morals demanded preventative measures. A paragraph in the statute book accused even parents of the punishable offence of procuring if they allowed young people under the age of 18 to spend a night together under their roof.

Education and upbringing were – and still are – concepts that leading politicians liked to talk a lot about. After all, the problem of a fundamental change of mindset was on the political agenda, with the aim of producing mature and responsible citizens. A man like the prime minister of Hesse, Georg August Zinn, demonstrated his commitment personally when he visited one of the new "centre schools" in the summer of 1956. The pupils' grandfathers probably sat at the same desks. And the majority of those serving as teachers were the same people that had propagated national socialist ideology under the "brown" dictatorship. Alternatives were few and far between as long as the replacements were still studying. Not infrequently, with apparently unexpected suddenness, the entirely foreseeable school leaving exams would interrupt what in most grammar schools was the sluggish flow of chronologically administered

history teaching, so that "First World War" and "Second World War" had to be rushed through in abbreviated form for the sake of duly fulfilling the requirements of the curriculum. Not a word about genocide. Could it be that one of the neatly barbered boys in the photograph with Hesse's head of government demonstrated twelve years later on the streets of Frankfurt and Berlin against the authority of the state, threw cobblestones and argued over the fine line between violence against property and violence against the person? The majority of 68ers did not "lead a crackbrained life", says actor Elmar Wepper, who was one of them. It is the possible, not the actual that bars the way to Utopia, according to Theodor W. Adorno, one of the fiercest and most brilliant critics of the bourgeois-capitalist social system. His views and the critical position of the Frankfurt School shaped over years the definitive image of the period of the economic miracle.

As a sharp-eyed observer, Darchinger gave vivid shape in his pictures to the mainstays of the social system in the Federal Republic: politics, industry, technology, consumerism and education. Culture proper is absent – except for a cabaret-style protest against German rearmament, a price that Chancellor Adenauer was prepared to pay for the – limited – sovereignty of the defeated and occupied country. Against the will of the majority of the people. The reason for the striking omission is on the one hand the assignments the photographer's profession required him to fulfil. He was often away on commissions for the Social Democratic Party. He put together informative slide shows with synchronized sound for briefing purposes and did portraits of party grandees for election campaigns, which gave him access to the political caste. He also produced postcards and took photographs in a variety of genres for all kinds of newspapers and illustrated magazines. On the other hand, the huge need felt in the immediate postwar period to make up for cultural deprivation had evaporated by the time the photographer began his unintended chronicle, and material interests had taken the place of cultural ones. Cinema flourished as never before and signalled a growing need for entertainment. In June 1956, a single hoarding in Cologne advertised four films, an art exhibition, dancing lessons, a political function and a "great battle day for boxing" featuring the popular middleweight Peter Müller or "Müllers Aap" as he was affectionately nicknamed in the vernacular because of his monkey face. The television conquered the living rooms and drove the radio from its central position. It would not only substantially transform the universe of images but by virtue of its pictures would also change the world and the behaviour of the people in it. A process that Darchinger's political photographs for *Der Spiegel* magazine (more intensively after 1964) and the weekly *Die Zeit* memorably illustrate.

The workers were the cornerstone of the economic upturn

Cultural circles in the Fifties largely saw themselves as a stronghold of opposition to the prevailing conditions in the country. The ruling CDU and their satellites were seen by many as too reactionary, the SPD opposition as too philistine. In return, the politicians in government would occasionally denounce the rebellious culture luminaries as "rats" or "blow-flies". It was only with the advent of Willy Brandt that relations changed fundamentally. Darchinger photographed the charismatic governing mayor of Berlin and new leader of the largest of the opposition parties on an election campaign tour at a specially organized event in Bayreuth in 1965, as he listened to the writer Günter Grass and other intellectuals holding forth.

It was with all the greater emphasis that the photographer focused on those factors that powered the economic recovery of the young Federal Republic of Germany and furnished them with unforgettable faces. The steelworkers at an iron foundry, the fitters, men and women, in the electrical industry, the printers operating the rotary press at a newspaper publisher's, the road menders who built the country's vital infrastructure with their antiquated tar spreaders, the miners below ground, who demonstrated above ground against the closure of their unprofitable pits, the shipyard workers and dockers in the port cities, the customer advisers in the mail-order firms – the chimneys are smoking again, people said, and almost everyone was happy about it. Some of the pictures are reminiscent of television films that were shot twenty years later, others are redolent of the spirit that influenced popular science-fiction series. The fiction compelled them willy-nilly and in hindsight under its sphere of influence.

Slaving away on Saturdays was normal; very little attention was paid to health and safety standards for workers. The resolve to clear up the proverbial mess united people, and the economic success that was becoming relatively quickly apparent reconciled people to the unaccustomed democratic way things were being run. There were quite a few at first who shared the view of Nobel laureate Thomas Mann, which the author had expressed in his much-quoted "Reflections of a Non-Political Man" (1918) long before the battle he waged against the Nazi dictatorship from his Californian exile: namely that "the much-decried 'authoritarian state'" is and remains the one that is proper and becoming to the German people. The authoritarian conduct of the business of government in the hands of Adenauer seemed to confirm the opinion of the writer. The more so as it was highly successful. And it made it possible for those who had not come into the world as unimpeachable democrats to undergo tacitly a change of mindset. Anyone looking closer, however, will see below the surface optimism a deeply

Italien, „das Land, wo die Zitronen blühen", lockte die Deutschen. Doch zunächst mussten sie ihre Sehnsucht symbolisch mithilfe schmalziger Schlager ausleben und ihre wenigen Urlaubstage vorwiegend im eigenen Land verbringen.
Haus der Geschichte, Bonn

Italy, "the land where the lemons grow", exercised a huge attraction for the Germans. But for the time being they had to live out their dreams with the help of schmaltzy pop songs and spend their scant holidays in their own country.
Haus der Geschichte, Bonn

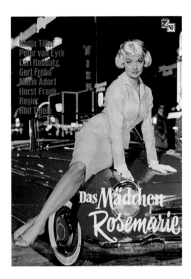

Den Mord an der Edelprostituierten Rosemarie Nitribitt in Frankfurt, ein früher Gesellschaftsskandal, nutzte das Kino zu einer Satire auf die Doppelmoral in den oberen Gesellschaftsetagen der Bundesrepublik. Unter der Regie von Rolf Thiele glänzte Nadja Tiller als „Das Mädchen Rosemarie". *1958*
Haus der Geschichte, Bonn

The murder of high-class call girl Rosemarie Nitribitt in Frankfurt, an early social scandal, was used by the cinema to satirize the double standards in the upper echelons of society in the Federal Republic. Under the direction of Rolf Thiele, Nadja Tiller gave a brilliant performance as "The Girl Rosemarie". *1958*
Haus der Geschichte, Bonn

contradictory reality. Decisive moves towards modernization and obstinate adherence to old traditions overlapped. Not even the use of colour can mask the clear fault lines. Increasing automation in industry and agriculture, technical advances in medicine, a rapid streamlining of bureaucracy came up against antiquated rituals in public life, private parochialism with the family gathered together in front of the new house altar, the television, and a strict hierarchy in such private and public institutions as family, school, university, administration and politics.

Women had to ask their husbands, if they wanted to go out to work

Of significance in this context is the role of women in the first years of the Federal Republic. Young women, often apostrophized as girls, learned to cook in domestic science classes at vocational school to fit them for running a household with a husband and children; others, it is true, learned hairdressing. In agriculture, all women, whatever their age, had to help with sowing and harvesting. After the currency reform in 1948, the women who had taken the place of the men in manufacturing and administration were ordered back into the kitchen. But economic prosperity with an average growth rate of 8.5 percent quickly led to a severe shortage of able-bodied workers. It opened up to them once more the doorway to areas of professional activity beyond the life of a housewife in tandem with a husband as propagated in German films and magazines. And it promised financial independence into the bargain. In 1955, women already accounted for a third of all people in employment. Married women still needed the permission of their husbands. Another flagrant inconsistency of the times was that women were not allowed to have a bank account, except with their husband's consent, and then he was allowed to pocket the interest.

The discordant notes sounded only subliminally. They showed up in nuances. But an attentive observer like Darchinger certainly did not fail to pick them up. When the notorious wave of gluttony started to roll, the fussily-stacked rows of canned foods in the delicatessens bore witness to a growing affluence. Ten years after the unconditional surrender of Nazi Germany, the shop windows were crammed full and basked in the superfluity of goods. Food out of a tin was the latest thing among higher earners; the obligatory prawn cocktail with pieces of the crustacean out of a can documented the high social prestige of whoever was the host. Food in cans also provided an infallible clue to the change in eating fashions in late modernism and a pointer to the gradual emancipation of women from the traditional drudgery of the kitchen. Out of the tin into the saucepan

and onto the table, was the motto in an increasing number of families. Interminable preparations were abandoned, and long-term stockpiling was also not a problem with canned food. Fresh foods, as everyone knows, only keep for a few days, and refrigerators, which have done more than all the other technological achievements together to bring lasting change to our daily lives and habits because they make it possible to lay in plenty of stocks, were still owned by only very few households. Against the backdrop of the colourful tin-can culture in the delicatessens, the seasonal sales in the downtown department stores, which had exiled to the outlying districts the traditional retail businesses with personal customer service, became a battle ground for people fighting over special offers and cut-price clothes. It was not only the people on the dark side of the economic miracle who braved the crowds for the sake of a bargain.

The Americanization of the Federal Republic proceeded imperceptibly but relentlessly. It happened first in the area of consumer behaviour. Darchinger highlighted its visible signals from time to time at focal points of interest. The trademark of the globally operating Coca-Cola company on Potsdamer Platz in Berlin in the immediate vicinity of the demarcation line. Or in the university canteens the typical glasses of the soft drinks firm whose products became the students' preferred choice. Even the neon lights of the big cities, which his photographs reproduce, imitated American models. Hollywood ousted the German film from its dominant position in German cinemas and expanded to the point where it had a virtual monopoly over German screens. And comics, pilloried by teachers as morally corrupting works of the devil, found their fans in the land of Wilhelm Busch and were read not only under the desk at school. American literature, too, in professional German translation, was published in large numbers of copies. Ernest Hemingway, William Faulkner, John Dos Passos and Thornton Wilder for the culturally highbrow, Dashiell Hammett, Raymond Chandler, Ross Macdonald and Mickey Spillane for aficionados of the detective genre. The publishing house Rowohlt, with its affordable paperback editions, was an important driving force. Three of the four "whodunit" authors have meanwhile achieved the status of high-calibre men of letters in Germany.

For young Germans, Kennedy was the embodiment of the hope for change

The years of the postwar era and the economic miracle were drawing to a close when the youthful Senator John F. Kennedy issued a challenge in the American elections to the distinctly unappealing Richard "Tricky Dicky" Nixon, who was vice-president in the ossified government of world-war general Dwight D. Eisen-

Der „Urwalddoktor" Albert Schweitzer
war in den 50er Jahren eine Art morali-
sche Instanz. In der heftigen Debatte
um die von Adenauer betriebene Atom-
bewaffnung der Bundeswehr ergriff er
Partei für deren Gegner. *1958*
Haus der Geschichte, Bonn

"Jungle Doctor" Albert Schweitzer
was a kind of moral authority in the
Fifties. In the fierce debate about
Adenauer's proposed arming of the
Bundeswehr with tactical nuclear weap-
ons, he was on the side of its opponents.
1958
Haus der Geschichte, Bonn

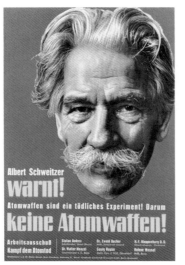

**Auch die DDR hatte ihr
Wirtschaftswunder,** allerdings weit
bescheidener als der westliche Nachbar.
Die Machthaber verbanden die Feier
des eigenen Erfolges mit der Propaganda
gegen die Bundesrepublik. *1950er Jahre*
Deutsches Historisches Museum, Berlin

**The GDR also had its economic
miracle.** Much more modest than that of
its Western neighbour. The ruling powers
there combined the celebration of their
own success with propaganda against the
Federal Republic. *1950s*
Deutsches Historisches Museum, Berlin

hower. To the generation of war children in the western world, he seemed to be
the living embodiment of the change everyone longed for; the promise of a fundamental shift in the direction of Western politics and liberation from the super-
annuated moral corset of the postwar period. In June 1963, two years after the
powers-that-be in the GDR had enclosed the east of Germany within a wall, he
would visit the Federal Republic as the President of the USA. Darchinger photographed him on his arrival, relaxed and carefree under the eye of his bodyguards.
No sign of the cordon sanitaire which half a century after his visit would shield
political notables from the crowds. In the marooned West Berlin, he won the
hearts of the people when he declared, "Ich bin ein Berliner". No one guessed
that he was a seriously ill man and a walking pharmacy. Only a few months
later, he would be murdered. Kennedy, who owed his victory in the American
elections to his refreshing youthfulness, to the beautiful and glamorous wife at
his side and the fact that he cut a better figure on television than his rival, com-
pletely rewrote the rules of politics despite the brevity of his time in office.
The undisguised liking for Kennedy in the young Germans was transferred to
Willy Brandt. He was soon the SPD's candidate for chancellor and threw his hat
in the ring, albeit in vain at first, against CDU patriarch Konrad Adenauer.
Darchinger provided the photographic accompaniment to a number of his campaign tours. The rides in an open car with curious children in tow instead of
suspicious "personal security agents", and the wildly acclaimed appearances in
the packed-out Westphalia Hall in Dortmund. Television presence and media-
genic appeal were not yet critical factors in deciding elections.
The worst blot on the West German success story of reconstruction, economic
recovery and international recognition eludes the evidence of photography. No
sooner had the Federal Republic achieved sovereignty at least in its internal
affairs than there was a slackening in the efforts to bring to trial the surviving
perpetrators of the "Third Reich" and see them justly punished. Their unimagi-
nable crimes were lost to sight. The bright colours of the economic miracle cov-
ered up the horror of the past. National Socialism and "total war" mutated in
the public mind into incomprehensible strokes of fate. Many of the significant
actors involved succeeded in fleeing abroad. A larger number managed to install
themselves in the public and private institutions of the new governmental system. One of the official commentators of the infamous Nuremberg race laws
even rose to become head of the Federal Chancellery and sat out all reproaches
until he reached retirement.
But it was not only people who were the brains behind the crimes who carried
on their earlier work unhindered in government administration, law, medicine,
the police, the media and the universities; many of the thugs and henchmen did

so too. "We didn't know", was the unison cry of the deeply embroiled when the
generation of 68ers asked their penetrating questions. They knew nothing of the
death camps and the war of extermination that was systematically carried out in
the east. As though their fellow citizens in Naziland were not publicly branded
with the yellow Nazi star, driven out of their houses and in the end crammed
into the cattle trucks of the railway; as though the endless wagons did not travel
over the tracks of the "Reich", and were not shunted off to wait for hours and
days in open country or in freight depots so that trains "vital to the war effort"
could pass. And the returning soldiers, who knew about the massacres, kept
silent like those who had stayed at home. Before this masking out of responsi-
bility for one's own history, the otherwise so meticulous photography of Josef
Heinrich Darchinger has to capitulate.

**Ein Schild, ein paar Pfähle, ein paar
Meter Stacheldraht:** die Zonengrenze
zwischen Deutschland West und
Deutschland Ost am Ostseestrand in
Travemünde. *1959*

**A sign, a few posts, a few metres of
barbed wire:** the inner-German border
between West and East Germany on the
Baltic shore in Travemünde. *1959*

Familienleben.
Der Herr im Haus bin ich

Family Life.
I am master in my own house

Der Vater war das Oberhaupt der Familie, seine Autorität trotz aller Wechsel-
fälle der Geschichte in der prosperierenden Bundesrepublik ungebrochen. Dabei
wuchsen viele Kinder ohne Väter auf. Die Väter waren im Krieg geblieben,
gefallen oder in Gefangenschaft. Schon während des Krieges hatten die Mütter
ihre Rolle übernehmen müssen. Als sie heimkehrten, reagierten viele Männer
irritiert. Doch selbst die Kinder, die vaterlos aufwuchsen, begegneten noch auf
Schritt und Tritt den autoritären Strukturen aus längst vergangener Zeit –
in der Verwandtschaft, in der Schule, der Lehre, auf der Universität und im
Beruf. Einer gab den Ton an, und fast immer war es ein Mann. Konrad
Adenauers autoritärer Regierungsstil passte ins Mentalitätsgefüge. Anfangs der
„Wirtschaftswunderzeit" waren Prügel gegen allzu aufmüpfige Sprösslinge
gebräuchlich – und erlaubt. Dennoch hatte das überkommene Familienbild
bereits tiefe Risse erhalten. Im Laufe der Jahre wurden sie immer tiefer. Alle
Versuche, die Frauen wieder an Küche und Kinderzimmer zu fesseln, scheiter-
ten. Empfehlungen in Handbüchern „für die gute Ehefrau", nichts unversucht
zu lassen, um dem Ehemann das Dasein so angenehm wie möglich zu gestalten,
wirkten angesichts eines Wirtschaftsbooms, der den Einsatz der Frauen im Beruf
energisch forderte, ebenso lächerlich wie hilflos. „Seien Sie glücklich, ihn zu
sehen", hieß es da. „Beklagen Sie sich nicht" oder „Schieben Sie ihm das Kissen
zurecht", lauteten weitere Gebote für die dienstbereite Gattin. Der Hinweis,
dass derlei und manches andere neben dem Kochen, Putzen und Aufräumen zu
„ihren Pflichten" gehöre, fehlte nicht. Gleichwohl war die gesetzliche Gleich-
stellung von Mann und Frau nicht mehr aufzuhalten. Realität und Ideologie
klafften mächtig auseinander. Während der 60er Jahre häuften sich auch die
Proteste der Jugend gegen die traditionelle Autorität der Väter. Sie äußerten sich
in wechselnden Formen. Zunächst fanden sie ihren Ausdruck in der populären
Musik sowie in unkorrekter Kleidung und ungewohntem Haarschnitt. Später
wurden bohrende Fragen an die Überlebenden gerichtet: „Was habt ihr im
Krieg gemacht?" Bisweilen antworteten die Autoritäten aggressiv. Die Proteste
verlagerten sich auf die Straße und gipfelten in einer Revolte.

The father was the head of the family. His authority remained unbroken irre-
spective of all the vicissitudes of history in the prospering Federal Republic.
There were many children, though, who grew up without a father. Their fathers
had not come back from the war. They had been killed or were prisoners of war.
The mothers had been forced to take over their role during the war. When they
returned home, many men reacted with vexation. But even children who had
grown up without a father still encountered at every turn the authoritarian
structures from a bygone age – in the wider family, at school, as apprentices, as
university students and at work. There was one person who called the tune, and
almost always it was a man. Konrad Adenauer's authoritarian style of government fitted in with the prevailing mindset. At the start of the "economic miracle
period" it was customary – and permissible – to spank an all too obstreperous
offspring. But deep cracks had already appeared in the traditional image of the
family, and they became ever deeper as the years went by. All attempts to banish
women once more to the kitchen and the nursery signally failed. Advice in man-
uals "for the good wife" to leave no stone unturned in the effort to make a husband's life as agreeable as possible appeared as ludicrous as it was untenable in
the face of the economic boom, which vigorously demanded that women should
go out to work. "Be happy to see him," the books said. "Don't complain" or
"Straighten the cushion behind him" were other tips for the willing wife. And it
was made quite clear that this sort of thing together with the cooking and clean-
ing and keeping things tidy was part of "your duties". Despite all this, there was
no preventing equal rights for men and women being granted by law. The gap
between reality and ideology was huge. During the Sixties, there was an increasing number of protests by young people against the traditional authority of their
fathers. These were expressed in a variety of ways. Popular music was an early
form of protest, as were sloppiness of dress and odd hairstyles. Later penetrating
questions began to be asked of the survivors: "What did you do in the war?"
Occasionally the answer given by the authorities was aggressive. The protests
shifted out onto the streets and culminated in a revolution.

**Für die meisten Kinder waren die Ruinen ein
Abenteuerspielplatz von allerhöchstem Reiz,**
streng verboten und – auch deshalb – voller
Verlockungen. *Bonn 1953*

**For most children, the ruins were an adventure
playground with huge appeal,** strictly out-of-bounds
and – partly for that reason – full of temptations. *Bonn
1953*

Öffentliche Wasserversorgung aus der Grund-wasserpumpe im rheinischen Eckendorf. Für die Menschen auf dem Lande hatte der Staat zunächst wenig Geld übrig. Manche Städter erinnerten sich an bisweilen zwiespältige Erfahrungen bei ihren Hamsterfahrten aufs Land unmittelbar nach dem Krieg, als die Not am größten war. Sie sahen keine Notwendigkeit, die Bauern zu unterstützen. *1955*

Public water supply from a standpipe in Eckendorf in the Rhineland. The government had not yet had much money to spare for people living in rural areas. Quite a lot of town folk recalled their mixed experiences during foraging expeditions to the countryside right after the end of the war, when their need was greatest, and felt no compulsion to help the farmers. *1955*

24

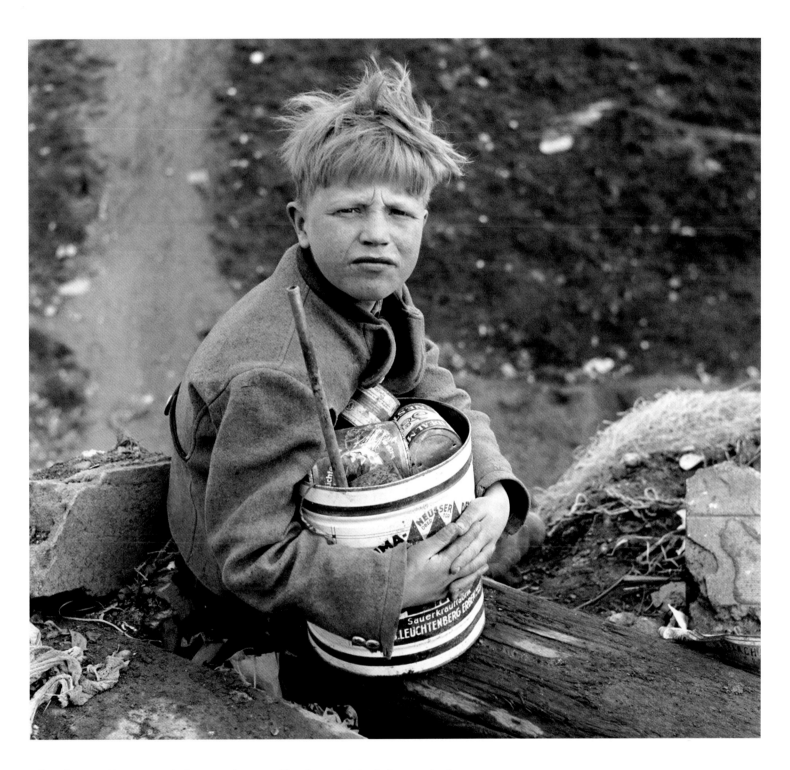

Schrott bringt Geld. Alteisen, auch Altpapier sind begehrte Handelswaren. Mancher Schrottkönig steigt schnell zum Millionär auf. Die Kinder aus der Notunterkunft Hermannshof in Bonn durchsuchen den Müll auf der städtischen Kippe gleich vor ihrer Barackentüre nach Alteisen, um die schmale Haushaltskasse aufzubessern. *1953*

There's money in trash. Scrap metal and waste paper, too, are sought-after commodities. Many a scrap-metal king becomes a millionaire in no time. The children from the Hermannshof hut camp in Bonn search through the trash at the municipal dump right at their door, looking for scrap metal to supplement the meagre family budget. *1953*

Barackenlager sind bis in die siebziger Jahre am Rand aller deutschen Städte ein gewohnter Anblick. Sie dienen als Notunterkünfte für Ausgebombte, Vertriebene und Flüchtlinge. 1948 kamen auf 14,6 Millionen Haushalte nur 9,4 Millionen Wohnungen. Der vom Staat massiv subventionierte soziale Wohnungsbau schafft langfristig Abhilfe. Bis 1956 werden zwei Millionen Wohnungen errichtet. Dennoch leben 11% der Arbeiterfamilien in Notunterkünften. *Bonn 1956*

Hut camps are a common sight on the outskirts of all German cities till well into the Seventies. They serve as temporary housing for people who have been bombed out, displaced persons and refugees. In 1948, for 14.6 million households, there were only 9.4 million homes. The social housing built with massive government subsidies provides long-term relief. By 1956, two million homes have been put up. But 11% of working-class families still live in makeshift accommodation. *Bonn 1956*

Zwei Mädchen aus einem Barackenlager in Bonn. Die Wohnungsnot war so groß, dass mancherorts wie in Dachau die Flüchtlinge in den Baracken eines Konzentrationslagers untergebracht wurden. *1954*

Two girls from a hut camp in Bonn. The housing shortage was so extreme that in some places – Dachau, for example – the refugees were housed in the huts of a concentration camp. *1954*

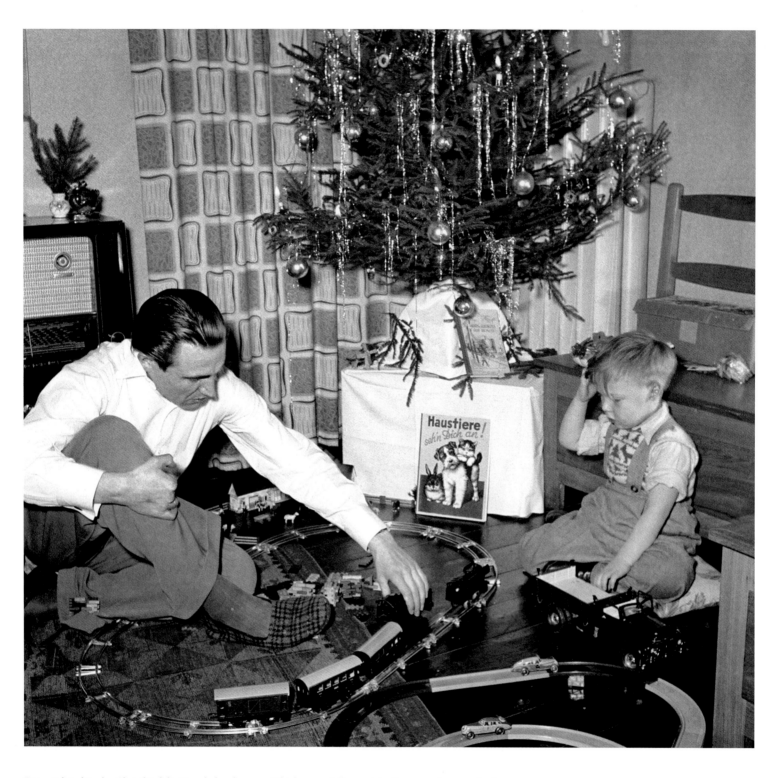

Für wen brachte das Christkind die Eisenbahn, den Traum fast aller Jungen? Weihnachten in Bonn. *1952*

Which one got the model railway, nearly every boy's dream, from Santa Claus? Christmas in Bonn. *1952*

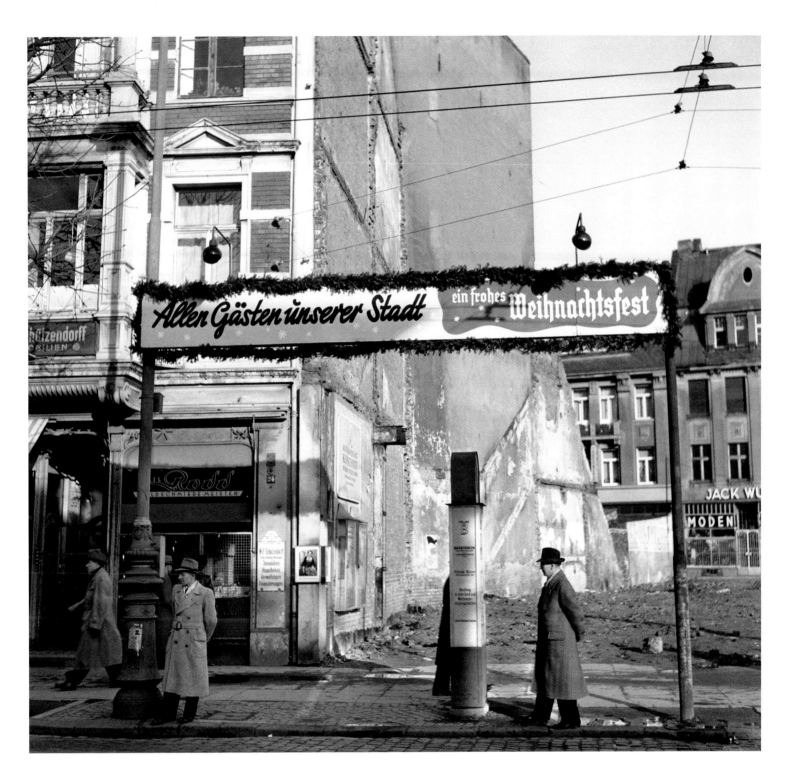

Freundliche Begrüßung am Hauptbahnhof der Bundeshauptstadt Bonn. 130 britische Bomber hatten die fast noch unzerstörte Stadt am 18. Oktober 1944 angegriffen. Es heißt, die Wirksamkeit eines neuen Navigationssystems zu demonstrieren sei ein Grund hierfür gewesen. Dazu bot eine weitgehend intakte Bebauung beste Voraussetzungen. Bonn kam glimpflich davon, nur 30 % der Stadt wurden zerstört. Angesichts der verwüsteten, aber schon aufgeräumten Stadt kommt die rechte Weihnachtsstimmung nicht auf. *25. Dezember 1952*

A warm welcome and Christmas greetings on a banner outside the main railway station in the federal capital of Bonn. 130 British bombers had attacked the city – till then virtually undamaged – on 18 October 1944, apparently to demonstrate the effectiveness of a new navigation system. A largely intact built-up area provided optimal test conditions. Bonn escaped lightly; only 30% of the city was destroyed. With the city so ravaged, even though the streets are now cleared, any real Christmas spirit remains elusive. *25 December 1952*

Unten:

Viele Tageszeitungen erscheinen mehrfach am Tag mit jeweils neuen Ausgaben. Wie die „Abendzeitung" in München und die Nachtausgabe der „Frankfurter Neuen Presse" in Frankfurt am Main. *1953*

Rechts:

Man traut sich zaghaft. Die Lichter gehen nach der Zeit erzwungener Verdunklung wieder an. Das graue Deutschland erhält ein paar neue Glanzlichter. Weihnachtsbeleuchtung in Essen. *1953*

Below:

Many daily newspapers put out new editions several times a day. Examples include the *Abendzeitung* in Munich and the late-night edition of the *Frankfurter Neue Presse* in Frankfurt/Main. *1953*

Right:

Confidence returns cautiously. The lights go on again after the years of enforced blackout. Grey Germany gets a few new highlights. Christmas illuminations in Essen. *1953*

OSRAM
Burgwallbronn
PHOTOGRAPHIERE MIT AGFA
NEUE RUHR-ZEITUNG
MÖBEL RAUMKUNST
EICK SÖHNE
FOTO Schmitter
Leica
ZEISS IKON
NEUE RUHR-ZEITUNG
Overbeck

Links:

In jahrelanger KZ-Haft als Kommunist hat er Gesundheit und Lebenskraft verloren. Seine Entschädigung: 95 DM Rente im Monat und ein Wohnraum in der Baracke in Bonn. Aber die Kommunistenjagd geht weiter. Zwischen 1951 und 1968 werden 138.000 Ermittlungsverfahren wegen „kommunistischer Umtriebe" eingeleitet. *1956*

Left:

Years of imprisonment in a concentration camp for being a communist have cost him his health and vigour. His compensation: a pension of 95 marks a month and accommodation in temporary housing in a camp in Bonn. But the hunt for communists goes on. Between 1951 and 1968, 138,000 preliminary proceedings are instigated on the grounds of "communistic activities". *1956*

Unten:

Reicht das Geld bis Monatsende? Ausgebombte Rentner mit ein paar geretteten Habseligkeiten und ihren Erinnerungsstücken in der Barackenunterkunft. An der Wand hängt ein Foto des vermissten Sohnes in der Uniform der U-Boot-Fahrer. *Bonn 1956*

Below:

Will the money last till the end of the month? Bombed-out pensioners with a few salvaged belongings and their keepsakes in temporary accommodation in a camp. Hanging on the wall is a photograph of their missing son in the uniform of a submariner. *Bonn 1956*

Mittagessen im Flüchtlingslager. Salzhering mit Pellkartoffeln und weißer Soße steht auf der Speisekarte in Wipperfürth. Über 2,7 Millionen Menschen verließen bis 1961 die DDR; die meisten nur mit Handgepäck. Sie wurden zunächst notdürftig versorgt. Da die aufblühende Wirtschaft Arbeitskräfte dringend brauchte, vollzog sich die Integration geräuschlos. *1956*

The midday meal in the refugee camp. Pickled herring with jacket potatoes and a white sauce is on the menu in Wipperfürth. Over 2.7 million left the GDR up to 1961, mostly just with hand luggage. They received only makeshift provision to start with. Since the booming economy urgently needed manpower, integration took place without a lot of fuss. *1956*

35

Links:

Der Menüzettel ist kurz, und viele Augen schauen in Mutters Kochtopf. Die schwierigen Verhältnisse, wie hier in einer Bonner Notunterkunft, stehen dem großen Kindersegen dieser Jahre nicht entgegen. *1956*

Left:

The menu is minimal, and there are a lot of eyes looking into mother's cooking pot. The difficult conditions, as here in an emergency shelter in Bonn, do not stand in the way of large numbers of children being born during these years. *1956*

Unten:

Wöchentlicher Badetag in der Wohnküche.
Wohnraum ist knapp und wird amtlich verwaltet. Eine große Wohnung verwandelt man in viele kleine. Badezimmer sind purer Luxus, selbst in Neubauten. Die Menschen schicken sich in das Unvermeidliche. *Bonn 1953*

Below:

Weekly bath day in the kitchen-cum-living-room.
Living space is in short supply and is managed by the authorities. A large flat is converted into a number of small ones. Bathrooms are a luxury, even in new buildings. People accept the inevitable. *Bonn 1953*

Oben:

Erster Schultag. Die Schule in Bonn ist zwar neu, aber viel zu klein. Im Rotationsverfahren vor- oder nachmittags nutzt jeweils eine andere Klasse denselben Schulraum. Man nennt das Schichtunterricht. *Bonn 1955*

Above:

First day at school. The school in Bonn is new but much too small. Different classes take turns to use the same room, mornings and afternoons. The system is known as teaching in shifts. *Bonn 1955*

Rechts:

Drei Mädchen auf einem Trümmergrundstück in Köln. *1956*

Right:

Three girls on a bomb site in Cologne. *1956*

Im Aufmarschgebiet gegen den Erzrivalen Frankreich hatte der Kaiser links des Rheins für seine Soldaten bauen lassen. Als Behelfsunterkunft für Ausgebombte und Flüchtlinge erfüllt die Kaserne des Bonner Husarenregiments doch noch einen guten Zweck. Bald weicht sie modernen Wohnhäusern. *1955*

When marshalling his resources against his arch-rival France, the Kaiser put up buildings for his troops on the left bank of the Rhine. As a makeshift shelter for refugees and people made homeless by the bombing, the barracks of Bonn's hussar regiment is finally put to good use. It will soon be demolished to make way for modern apartment blocks. *1955*

Kinderschar in der Kölner Altstadt. An gleichaltrigen Spielgefährten mangelte es nirgends, denn die Nachkriegsjahrgänge waren ungewöhnlich zahlreich. Über die Ursachen grübeln die Soziologen. Sicherlich hat die zuversichtliche Aufbruchsstimmung des Neuanfangs mitgeholfen. Der ‚Babyboom' war Mitte der sechziger Jahre auch schon wieder zu Ende, noch bevor die Antibabypille nennenswerte Verbreitung gefunden hatte. *1956*

Children galore in Cologne's old town. Thanks to a steep rise in birth rates after the war there was never a shortage of playmates. Sociologists brood over the causes. The general atmosphere of renewal certainly played a part. But the "baby boom" had subsided by the mid-Sixties, even before the contraceptive pill could come into full effect. *1956*

Oben:
Ein Spiel zum Erntedankfest. Der Bonner Kindergarten, provisorisch in einer Wehrmachtsbaracke untergebracht, ist restlos überbelegt. Im Hintergrund glüht ein großer silberfarbener Kohleofen. *1952*

Above:
A play for harvest festival. Temporarily housed in an army hut, the Bonn kindergarten is hopelessly overcrowded. The bright silver object in the background is a large coal-fired stove. *1952*

Rechts:
Schulkinder in Bremen beim Puppentheater. Ein Spiel über richtiges Verhalten im Verkehr. Der Mineralölkonzern Shell sorgt vor und trägt die Kosten. Fußgänger leben gefährlich, die Zahl der Unfälle wächst dramatisch. Über 350.000 Personenwagen befahren wieder die westdeutschen Straßen, von den Lastwagen, Omnibussen und Motorrädern zu schweigen. Die blonden Jungen am rechten Bildrand interessieren sich mehr für den Fotografen als für das Spiel. *1955*

Right:
School children in Bremen enjoying a puppet show. A piece about the right way to behave in traffic. Initiator and funder is the Shell oil company. Pedestrians live dangerously. The number of accidents is rising dramatically. Over 350,000 cars are driving again on West German roads, not to speak of the lorries, buses and motorbikes. The fair-haired boys on the far right of the picture are more interested in the photographer than in the play. *1955*

Seite 44/45:
Der Roller gehört zu einem Jungen wie der Kurz-haarschnitt – die Mienen zeigen es. Gleiches gilt für die Lederhose. Sie ist pflegeleicht, da nicht zu waschen. Je speckiger das Leder, desto mehr Prestige. In einer weichen Stoffhose wird keiner Anführer. *Bonn 1955*

Page 44/45:
A scooter's what a boy has to have, and a short hair-cut – it's written all over their faces. The same is true of the leather shorts. They are easy-care, never need wash-ing. The shinier the leather, the greater the prestige. No one gets to be leader in soft cloth pants. *Bonn 1955*

„Auto!", brüllt einer. Die Spielfläche muss kurzfristig geräumt werden. Da dies selten der Fall ist, fühlt sich nie-mand sonderlich gestört. *Bonn 1955*

Someone shouts "car". The playing area has to be cleared briefly. As this is a rare event, no one particularly minds. *Bonn 1955*

Für einen Groschen (10 Pfennig) gibt es ein Stück vom Paradies: eine Stange mit fünf Karamellbonbons. Wunderbar klebrig, verführen sie zum Kauen und ziehen dummerweise auch Plomben und lose Zähne. *Bonn 1955*

For a Groschen (10 pfennigs) you can buy a bit of heaven: a roll of five caramel toffees. Wonderfully sticky, it's hard not to chew them and unfortunately they can pull out fillings and loose teeth. *Bonn 1955*

Hamburg, im Gängeviertel. Kinder in den Hausein-
gängen der schlichten Backsteingebäude. Bald verschwin-
den die Arbeiterhäuser, Inbegriff frühkapitalistischen
Elends in einem berüchtigten Teil von St. Pauli. *1957*

Hamburg, in the old-city "lanes" quarter. Children in
the doorways of the simple brick buildings. These working men's houses will soon disappear. The epitome of
early capitalist penury in a notorious part of St. Pauli. *1957*

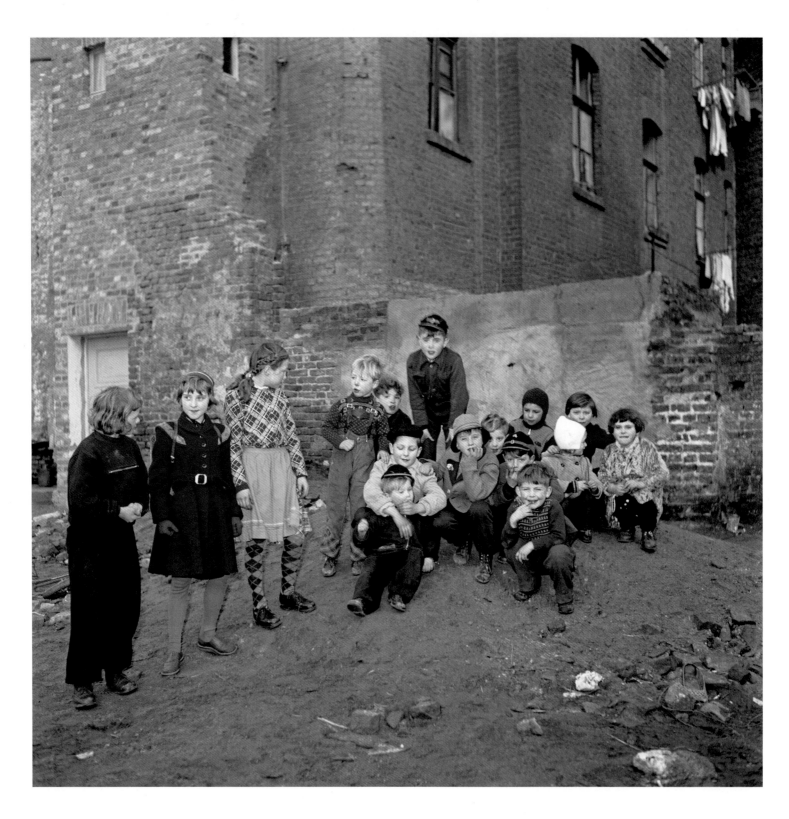

Köllsche Pänz in einem Hinterhof. Sie stehen auf dem Schutt von 2.000 Jahren Geschichte, die oberste und dickste Schicht ist gerade gut zehn Jahre alt. Dass diese Trümmerschicht für viele Jahrzehnte die letzte blieb, ist das ungeheure Glück der Nachkriegsgeneration. *1956*

Local children in a yard behind the houses in Cologne. They are standing on the debris of 2,000 years of history; the top layer and the thickest is just about ten years old. It is the great good fortune of the postwar generation that this layer remained the last for many decades. *1956*

Die US-amerikanische CARE-Mission beendete ihre Nahrungsmittelhilfe für Deutschland. CARE-Pakete haben die Beziehungen vieler Deutscher zu den USA außerordentlich positiv gestaltet. Zwischenzeitlich haben sich die materiellen Verhältnisse entscheidend verbessert. *Bonn 1957*

The US-American CARE mission ended its food aid to Germany. CARE packages had a highly positive impact on the feelings of many Germans towards the USA. Material circumstances have improved considerably in the meantime. *Bonn 1957*

Ein neuer Kindergarten in Hessen.
1956

A new kindergarten in Hesse.
1956

Händewaschen als Gemeinschaftserlebnis in Hessen – auch im Detail bricht sich der gesellschaftliche Fortschritt Bahn. *1956*

Hand washing as a shared experience in Hesse – social progress forges ahead even in the small details. *1956*

Mittagsruhe in einem Bremer Kindergarten mit
Ganztagsbetreuung. *1956*

An afternoon sleep in a Bremen kindergarten with
all-day care. *1956*

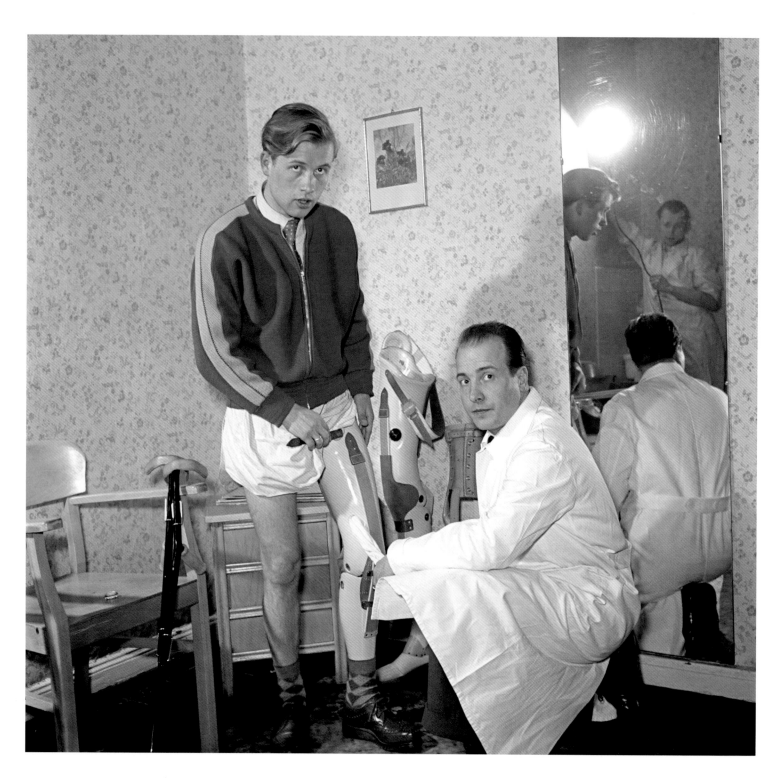

Ein Orden aus Blech, ein Bein aus Holz – das ist der
Dank des Vaterlandes. Beim Prothesenmacher in Bonn.
1956

A tin medal and a wooden leg – the thanks you get
from the fatherland. At the artificial limb maker's in
Bonn. *1956*

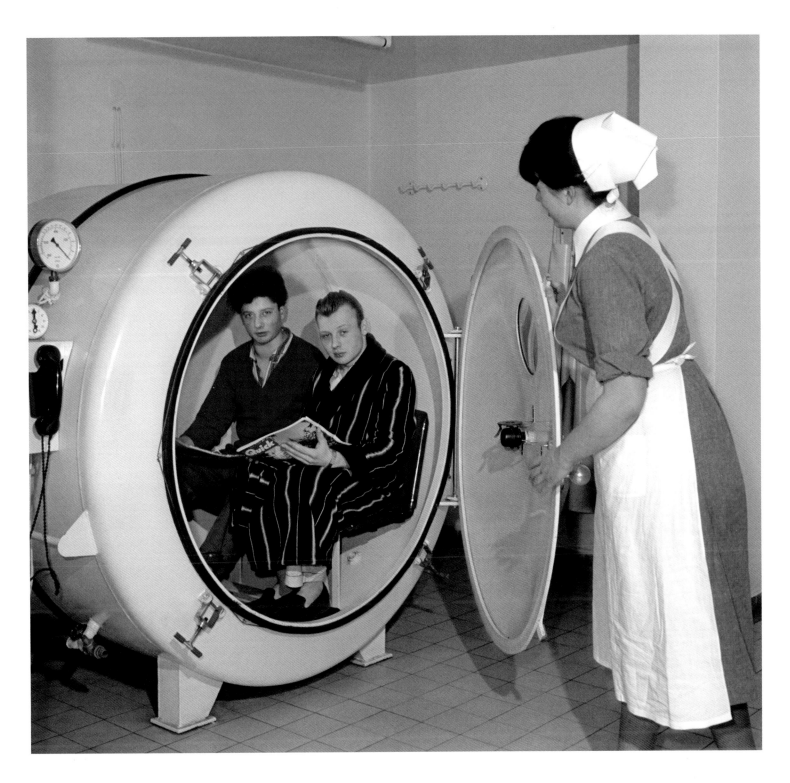

Keine Patientenwaschmaschine, sondern eine Unterdruckkammer. Die Leistungen der Krankenkassen werden laufend verbessert, sodass immer mehr Menschen vom technischen Fortschritt in der Medizin profitieren können. *Marl 1959*

Not a washing machine for patients but a decompression chamber. The provisions of the medical insurance companies are continually improving, so more and more people are able to benefit from technological advances in medicine. *Marl 1959*

Darf's ein bisschen mehr sein? Aufschnittplatten in der Küche. Vor den Büffets der vielen Empfänge herrscht heftiges Geschiebe und Gedränge. Die Gäste stopfen sich die Köstlichkeiten in den Mund, als wären sie Kleinkinder. Die Wissenschaft kennt das Verhalten als Klüver-Bucy-Syndrom. *1963*

Do you mind if it's a bit over? Plates of cold cuts in the kitchen. At the numerous receptions, there's a lot of pushing and shoving at the tables where the buffet is laid out. The guests cram the delicacies into their mouths just like small children. The scientific term for this is Klüver-Bucy syndrome. *1963*

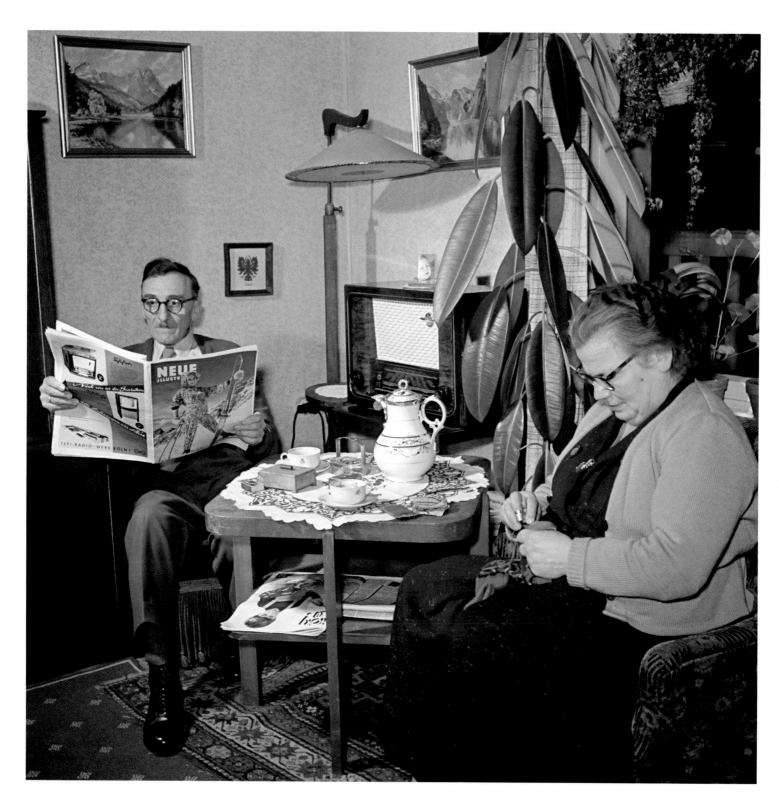

Endlich Feierabend. Mutter stopft Strümpfe, Vater liest eine illustrierte Zeitschrift. Die Eltern des Fotografen im Wohnzimmer ihrer kleinen Mansardenwohnung in Bonn. Selbst neue, öffentlich geförderte Sozialwohnungen haben nur eine Durchschnittsgröße von 50 Quadratmetern mit Toilette auf dem Flur. *1955*

The working day is over at last. Mother darns socks, Father reads an illustrated magazine. The photographer's parents in the living room of their small attic flat in Bonn. Even new, publicly subsidized council flats have an average size of 50 square metres with a WC on the landing. *1955*

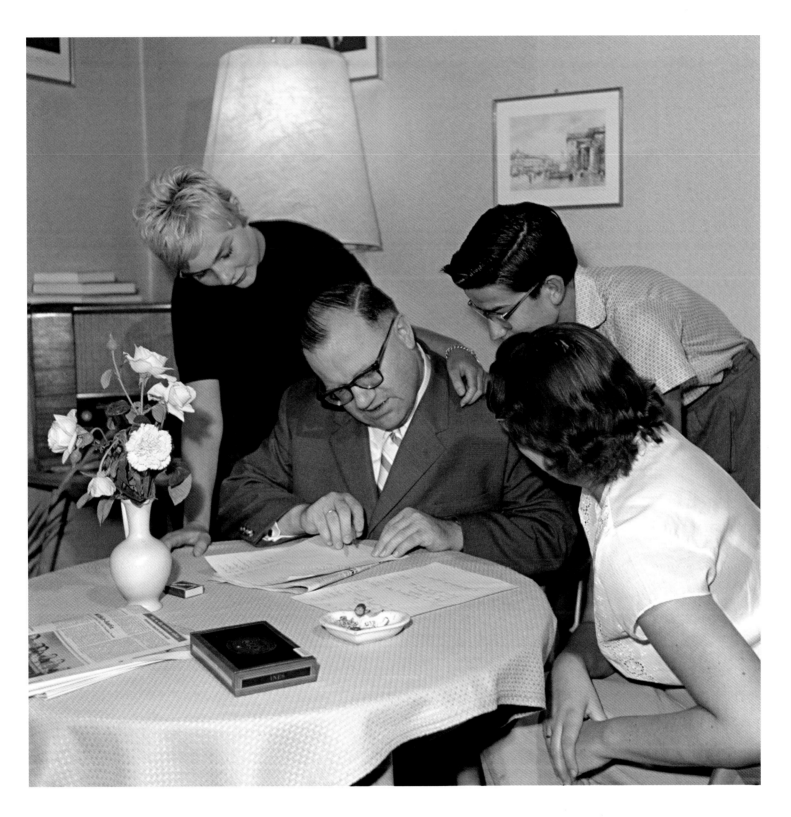

Familienkonferenz in einem Bonner Haus.
Ob über Zeugnisnoten oder die Anschaffung eines
Fernsehgerätes diskutiert wird, ist nicht überliefert. *1957*

Family conference in a house in Bonn.
Whether about school results or the purchase
of a TV set is not recorded. *1957*

Das große Wunder Fernsehen. Ab 1956 eröffnet die „Tagesschau" aus Hamburg das Gemeinschaftsprogramm der westdeutschen Sender. Es dauert in der Regel bis 22 Uhr. Einen Fernseher können sich noch nicht alle leisten. Entsprechend groß ist der Zuspruch in Kneipen oder wie hier im „Dorfgemeinschaftshaus", einer Einrichtung zur Bildung genossenschaftlicher Strukturen in der Landwirtschaft. Das kitschige Wandgemälde illustriert den Ursprung dieser Idee. Dank der Fußballweltmeisterschaft 1954 gibt es schon rund 60.000 Fernsehapparate im Westen. *Fritzlar, Hessen, 1956*

The miracle of television. From 1956, the "Tagesschau" news from Hamburg opened the programme that is broadcast simultaneously by all the West-German stations. This usually lasts until 10 pm. Not everyone can afford a television yet, so a lot of people watch it in pubs, or as here in the "village assembly rooms", an amenity set up to create co-operative structures in farming. The kitschy mural illustrates the origin of this idea. Thanks to the Football World Cup in 1954, there are already about 60,000 TV sets in the West. *Fritzlar, Hesse, 1956*

Dörfliche Stammtischrunde beim Frühschoppen im Taunus. *1960*

A table reserved for regulars enjoying a pint in a village pub in the Taunus region. *1960*

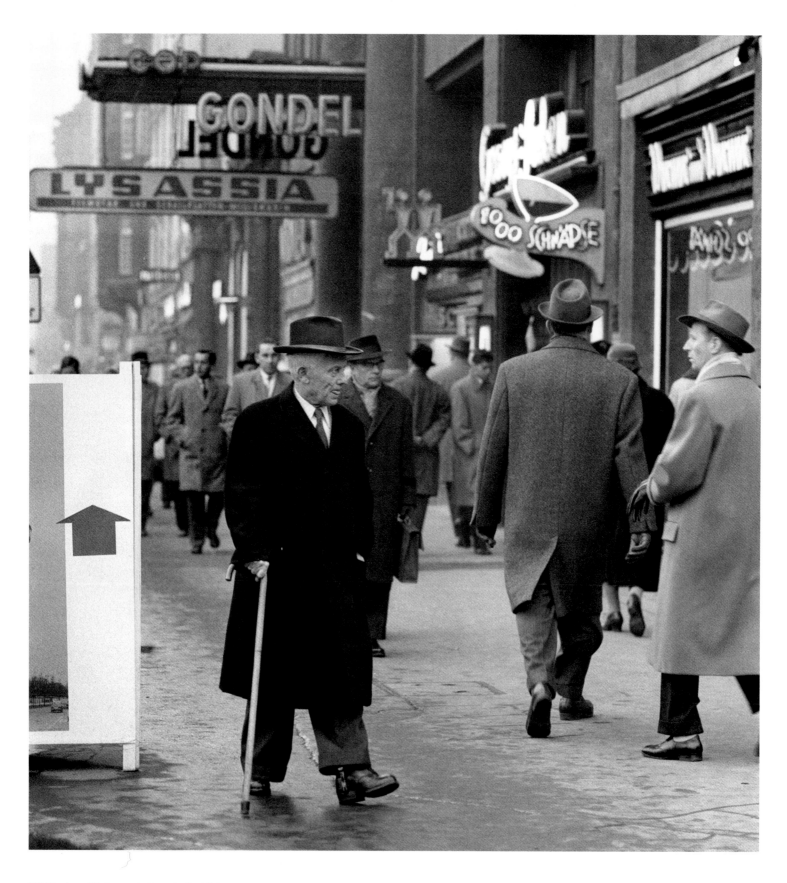

Mit Stock und Hut – es gab sie noch, die sichtbaren Attribute der sozial Bessergestellten. Und die Herren, die dazu passten. *Hannover 1960*

With hat and stick – they were still around, the visible attributes of the socially better off. And the gentlemen who went with them. *Hanover 1960*

In der beinahe mediterranen Stadtkulisse Hannovers zwei Rollstuhlfahrer mit ihren sperrigen dreirädrigen Gefährten, die kein Verkehrsmittel aufnehmen konnte. Kriegsversehrte sind ein selbstverständlicher Bestandteil des Straßenbildes. Im Unterschied zu den Eigenkonstruktionen aus Brettern gelten diese Rollstühle als komfortable Vehikel. *1960*

Set against the almost Mediterranean cityscape of Hanover: two wheelchair users with their unwieldy three-wheeled conveyances, which no type of public transport could accommodate. Disabled ex-servicemen are a not unusual sight on the streets. Compared with the home-made contraptions built from planks, these wheelchairs are considered comfortable vehicles. *1960*

Schuhe zu Ramschpreisen. Auch in Bonn geht der Handel neue Wege und modernisiert seine Verkaufsflächen. Die Aktion weist auf den kommenden Überfluss voraus. *1954*

Shoes at knock-down prices. In Bonn, too, the retail trade is breaking new ground and modernizing its selling space. The move prefigures the affluence to come. *1954*

Als es zum ersten Mal in die Schule geht, Einschulung
heißt das im Bürokratendeutsch, müssen neue Schuhe her.
Bonn 1955

When it's time to start school, a child needs new shoes.
Bonn 1955

Peter Müller, als „Müllers Aap" populärer Kölner Mittelgewichtschampion, boxt gegen Janssens aus Belgien. „Lügen haben hübsche Beine", im Film. „Das Liebesmanöver" mit Brigitte Bardot, der freizügigeren französischen Antwort auf Marilyn Monroe. Ein Vortrag von Professor Dr. Friedensburg zum Tag der deutschen Einheit. Tanzkurse für die Freizeit. Der Maler Robert Delaunay im Museum Leverkusen – Events der Zeit: Plakatanschlag in Köln. *1956*

Peter Müller, a.k.a. "Müllers Aap", a popular middle-weight champion from Cologne, is boxing against Janssens from Belgium. "Lies Have Long Legs" – in film. "Summer Manoeuvres" with Brigitte Bardot, France's answer to Marilyn Monroe, only even sexier. A lecture by Professor Friedensburg on the Day of German Unity. Dancing classes. A Robert Delaunay exhibition at the Leverkusen Museum. Events of the day: poster hoarding in Cologne. *1956*

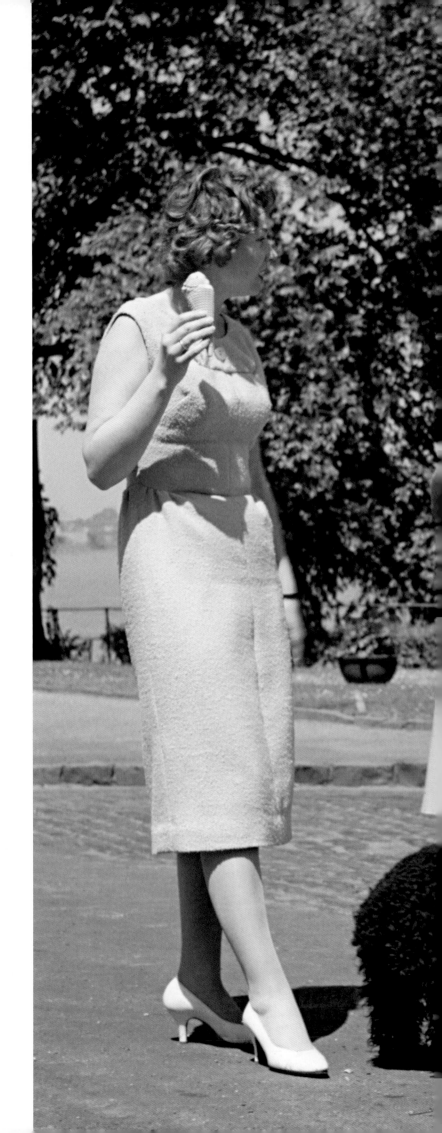

Am Rheinufer in Bonn. *1959*

On the bank of the Rhine in Bonn. *1959*

Karnevalistischer Klamauk vor dem Dom in Köln als Wahlkampfattraktion. Man suchte noch nach dem passenden Format. *1953*

Carnivalesque tomfoolery as an electioneering stunt in front of the cathedral in Cologne. They just needed to find the right format. *1953*

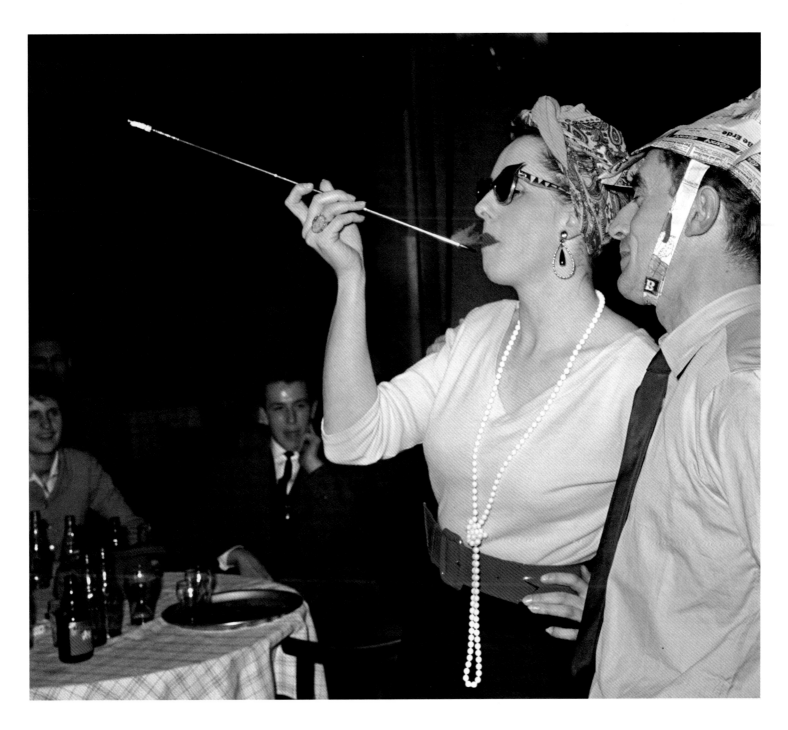

Kabarett in einer Hamburger Kneipe. Die imponierende Kopfbedeckung des Herrn erlaubt kein Missverständnis: Zielscheibe der Wortattacken ist das Militär! Die Mehrheit der Deutschen lehnt die von der Bundesregierung betriebene Wiederbewaffnung, politischer Preis für die Zuerkennung begrenzter Souveränität, strikt ab. *1956*

Cabaret in a Hamburg pub. The gentleman's impressive headgear admits of no misunderstanding: the target of the verbal assaults is the military! The majority of Germans are categorically opposed to the government's policy of rearmament, the political price for being granted limited sovereignty. *1956*

Das Kaffeekränzchen ist Bestandteil eines gehobenen Lebensstandards, ebenso die Zigarette und das farbige Geschirr in hochmodernem Design. In einer Umfrage sprachen sich 50% der Menschen für eine moderne Wohnungseinrichtung im Bauhausstil aus. *Bonn 1958*

Inviting the girlfriends around for coffee is an essential part of a sophisticated life style; likewise the cigarette and the colourful china in the latest design. An opinion poll put 50% of people in favour of a modern home-furnishing style in the Bauhaus manner. *Bonn 1958*

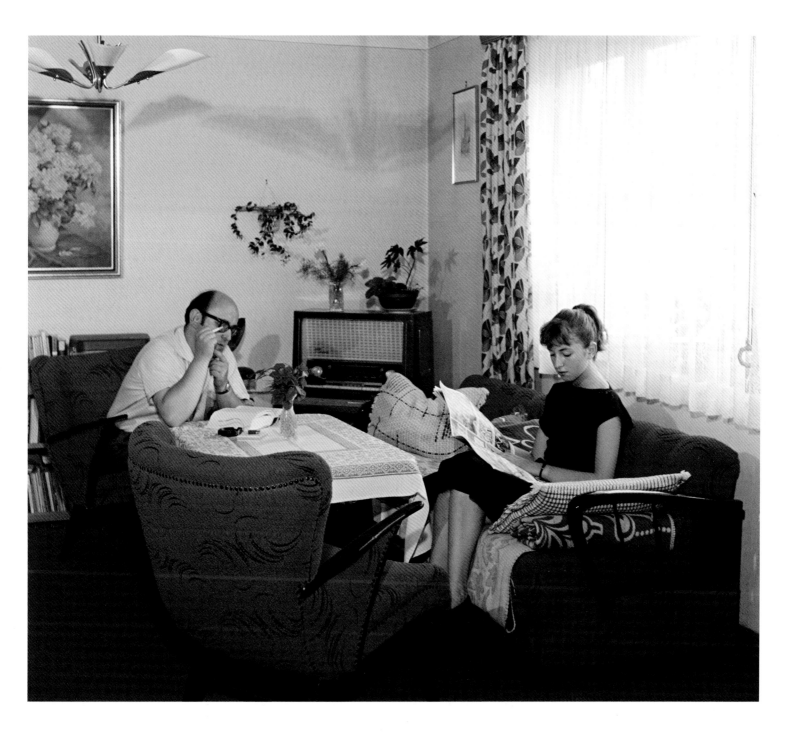

Zeitungslektüre im Wohnzimmer. Noch hat das Radio seinen zentralen Platz. Der Rundfunk leistete einen wichtigen Beitrag zur neuen Zivilität der Deutschen. *Bonn 1958*

Reading the newspaper in the living room. The wireless still retains its central position. Radio broadcasts made an important contribution to the new civility of Germans. *Bonn 1958*

Unten:

Zu Unrecht vermisst man ein vergleichbares Mess-gerät für den Verstand. Denn – einem Satz von Albert Einstein zufolge – es glaubt ohnehin jeder, er hätte genug davon. Jahrmarkt in Neuss. *1961*

Below:

It's a mistake to think we ought to have a machine to measure intelligence like this one for measuring strength. Because according to Albert Einstein, we're all convinced we have enough of it anyway. A funfair in Neuss. *1961*

Rechts:

Menschenmassen auf der Wies'n beim Oktoberfest in München. *1960*

Right:

Crowds on the Theresienwiese at the Oktoberfest in Munich. *1960*

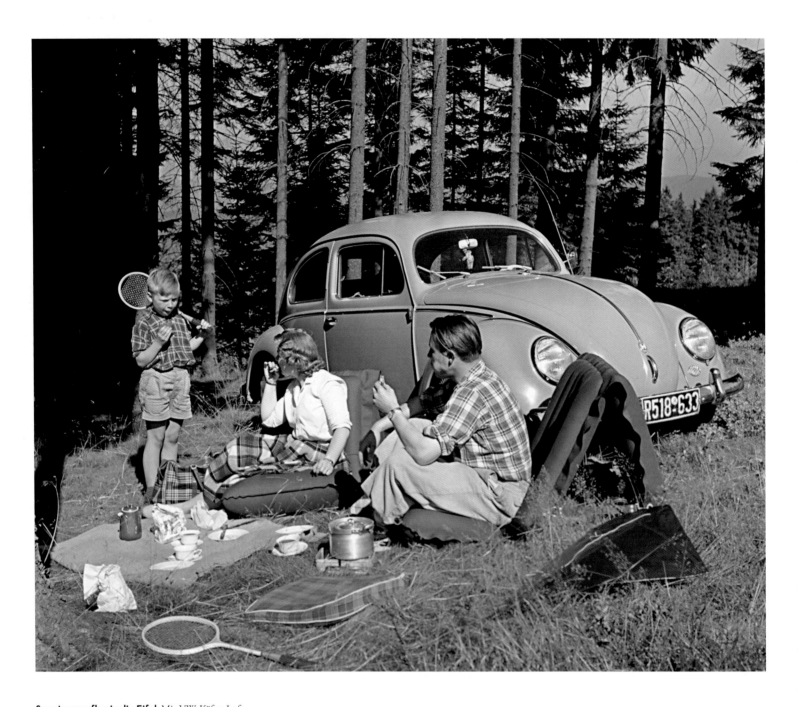

Sonntagsausflug in die Eifel. Mit VW-Käfer, Luft-
matratzen und Federballspiel ins Grüne. *1957*

A Sunday out in the Eifel. A trip to the countryside in
the VW Beetle, with inflatable mattresses and badminton
racquets. *1957*

Sonntagsausflug. Der Wohlstand wächst, und man fährt komfortabler. *1958*

A Sunday in the country. Affluence is on the increase and cars are getting more comfortable. *1958*

Rast bei einer Wanderung im Allgäu.
1963

Taking a rest on a walk in the Allgäu.
1963

Ansturm auf die Gipfel. Oberbayern ist nach wie vor
das beliebteste Urlaubsziel der Deutschen. *1959*

Stampede for the peaks. Upper Bavaria continues
to be the Germans' favourite vacation spot. *1959*

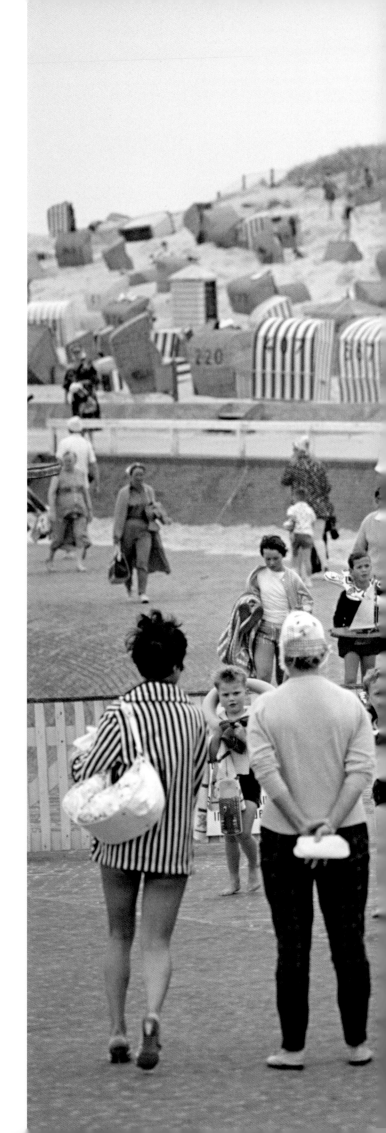

Strandurlaub auf Norderney. Noch ist die Nordseeinsel ein beliebtes Urlaubsziel. Doch schon 1962 befördert die Fluggesellschaft Condor 32.000 Urlauber nach Mallorca. Die Baleareninsel wird alle deutschen Inseln im Zuspruch der Urlauber rasch überflügeln. *1960*

Seaside holiday on Norderney. The island in the North Sea is still a popular holiday resort. But in 1962, Condor Airlines are already flying 32,000 holidaymakers to Majorca. The Balearic island will rapidly outstrip all the German islands in popularity. *1960*

Die prächtigen Bürgerhäuser vor dem Bonner Bahnhof säumen noch nach dem Ende des Krieges die Poststraße. Anfang der siebziger Jahre fallen sie der Spitzhacke zum Opfer. Der Modernisierungswahn der Stadtoberen beschert den Bürgern an ihrer Stelle das berüchtigte „Bonner Loch", den Ein- und Ausgang zum unterirdischen Teil des Bahnhofs. Auf der anderen Seite eine mit umlaufenden Stegen verblendete Blechschachtel im modernistischen Outfit. Manche behaupten, in der Nachkriegszeit seien mehr Häuser zerstört worden als im Krieg. *1955*

The splendid town houses across from the railway station in Bonn still line the Poststraße after the end of the war. In the early Seventies they fall prey to the pickaxe. The craze for modernization that possessed the city fathers gives the citizens the infamous "Bonn Hole" in their place, the entrance and exit to the underground part of the railway station. On the other side, a tin box in modernist get-up faced with horizontal fluting. It is widely claimed that more houses were destroyed in the post-war period than during the war itself. *1955*

Hamburg, Mönckebergstraße. Die Lücken, die der Bombenhagel schlug, wurden durch schlichte Neubauten geschlossen. Sie entsprachen der ästhetischen Doktrin, die sich auf die unterbrochene Tradition des Bauhauses berief. Die Straßen füllten sich mit Passanten und Kauflustigen. *1955*

Hamburg, Mönckebergstraße. The gaps that opened up under the hail of bombs have been filled by plain new buildings. They followed the aesthetic doctrine that claimed to continue the interrupted tradition of the Bauhaus. The streets bustled with passers-by and shoppers. *1955*

Schallplatten sind teuer und bei Jugendlichen sehr begehrt. Billige Kopien der angesagtesten Titel herzustellen ist nicht möglich. Erst als Tonbandgeräte erschwinglich werden, stellt die Reproduktion kein Problem mehr dar. Straßenhändler mit gebrauchten Schallplatten in Hamburg. *1960*

Left:

Records are expensive and highly prized by the young. There's no way of producing cheap copies of the hottest titles. Not until tape recorders become affordable does reproduction start being a problem. Street traders with second-hand records in Hamburg. *1960*

Unten:

Kippe an der Lippe und Frisur nach James-Dean-Art: Die Industrie hilft mit schrillem Outfit, schicken Mopeds und anderem Zubehör. Eine Kulturrevolution bahnt sich an. Das bürgerliche Wertesystem gerät allmählich ins Wanken. *Dortmund 1959*

Below:

A cigarette dangling from the lips and a James Dean haircut: industry helps with the loud outfits, smart mopeds and other accessories. A cultural revolution is in the wind. The system of middle-class values is beginning to totter. *Dortmund 1959*

Links:
Alle Menschen sollen es schön haben.
Bundesgartenschau im Westfalenpark, einem ehemaligen
Zechengelände in Dortmund. *1961*

Left:
Something beautiful for everyone to enjoy: the
Federal Horticulture Show in Westphalia Park, an old
colliery site in Dortmund. *1961*

Unten:
**Die Kunst dem Volke — hier wird der Ausspruch
wahr.** Dass Provinzialität und Weltläufigkeit ein Widerspruch sind, ist sichtbar widerlegt. Kirmesstand in Bonn.
1961

Below:
**Art should be for the people — here the aspiration is
a reality.** That there is necessarily a contradiction
between the provincial and the cosmopolitan is clearly
refuted here. A stall at the funfair in Bonn. *1961*

Bandenkrieg im Sandkasten. *1960*

Gang warfare in the sandpit. *1960*

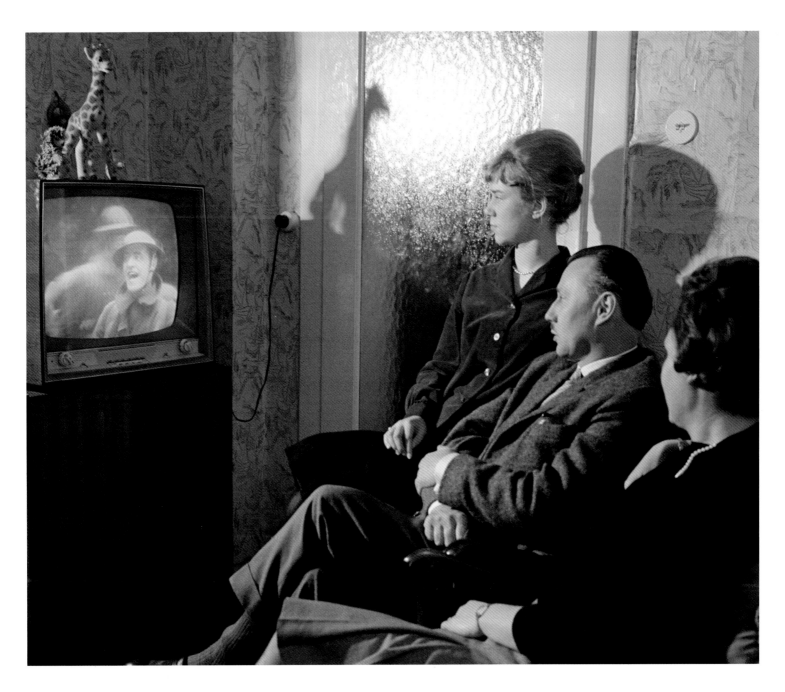

Das Fernsehen tritt seinen Siegeszug in den deutschen Wohnzimmern an. Das Programmangebot verdoppelt sich in den sechziger Jahren. Das Fernsehen wird zum Leitmedium. Die ARD mit ihren regionalen Programmen und seit 1963 das ZDF teilen sich die Kanäle. Der mehrteilige Krimi „Das Halstuch" von Francis Durbridge ist der „Straßenfeger" des Jahres. 1961 sind fünf Millionen Geräte angemeldet, 1970 werden es 16 Millionen sein. *1962*

Television begins its triumphal march through German living rooms. The choice of programmes doubles in the Sixties. TV takes over as the lead medium channelling social communication. The ARD with its regional programmes and from 1963 the ZDF share the channels. The Francis Durbridge thriller serial, "The Scarf", is the smash hit of the year. In 1961 five million sets are licensed, in 1970 there will be 16 million. *1962*

Oben:
Coca-Cola muss es sein. Kein anderes Konsumprodukt enthält so viel verlockende und fortschrittliche amerikanische Lebensart. Schmecken kann man die aber nicht. *Güdingen 1960*

Above:
Coca-Cola is a must. No other consumer product contains so much alluring and progressive American lifestyle. Not that you can taste it. *Güdingen 1960*

Rechts:
Animierende Umgebung statt Paukkaserne: Pausenraum in einem neuen Schulgebäude in Güdingen. Nachdem Aufnahmeprüfung und Schulgebühren abgeschafft worden sind, erlebt das Gymnasium einen großen Aufschwung. *1963*

Right:
Stimulating surroundings rather than a swot shop: break room in a new school building in Güdingen. After the abolition of entrance exams and school fees, grammar schools enjoy a considerable boom. *1963*

**Selbst anpacken heißt die Devise bei diesen Sied-
lungshäuschen im Saarland** – klein, aber mein, Haupt-
sache erschwinglich. Seit dem 1. Januar 1957 ist das
Saarland politisch, seit 1959 auch wirtschaftlich in die
Bundesrepublik eingegliedert. Bis dahin war es – eine
Folge des Krieges – in den französischen Wirtschaftsraum
einbezogen. *1960*

**Do it yourself is the motto with these little houses
on an estate in Saarland** – small but my own, the main
thing is that it's affordable. Since 1st January 1957,
Saarland has been politically integrated into the Federal
Republic and since 1959 it has also been economically
integrated. Up to then – as a consequence of the war –
it was part of France's economic territory. *1960*

Nicht schöner, aber besser wohnen – und bezahlbar. Staatliche Finanzierung mit dem programmatischen Namen sozialer Wohnungsbau macht dies möglich. Bis 1959 sind dank der staatlichen Initiative drei Millionen neue Wohneinheiten gebaut worden. Statistisch vergrößerte sich der Wohnraum für eine vierköpfige Familie von drei auf vier Zimmer. *Bremen 1962*

Living not more attractively but better – and at an affordable price. State funding with the programmatic title of subsidized housing makes it possible. By 1959, thanks to a government initiative, three million new housing units have been built. Statistically, the living space for a family of four increased from three rooms to four. *Bremen 1962*

Unten:

Neue Wohnungen werden fast immer in großen Baukomplexen am Rande der Städte gebaut. Wegen der modernen Ausstattung wie Zentralheizung und Warmwasserversorgung sind sie zunächst sehr beliebt. *1960*

Below:

New homes are almost always built in large complexes on the periphery of the towns. Modern amenities like central heating and hot-water supply make them very popular at first. *1960*

Rechts:

Rund um die großen Städte entstehen große Neubausiedlungen als reine Wohnanlagen.
Schlafstädte, schimpfen Kulturkritiker. Alles für das Leben unmittelbar Notwendige ist vorhanden, aber Urbanität und Ablenkung fehlen. Fahrten in überfüllten Vorortzügen und auf verstopften Straßen fördern die abendliche Unternehmungslust auch nicht gerade. 18 % Berufspendler zählte man 1950 und 31 % anno 1960, Tendenz steigend. *Stadtteil Neue Vahr in Bremen, 1962*

Right:

Around the periphery of the major cities, large new estates are built as purely residential complexes.
Dormitory towns, scorn the culture critics. The immediate necessities of life are all there, urbanity and distraction are not. Travelling on overcrowded suburban trains and congested roads doesn't exactly enhance the prospect of an evening out, either. 18% of people commuted to work in 1950 and 31% in 1960, and numbers are set to grow. *The Neue Vahr district in Bremen, 1962*

Links:

Der Idealtypus der Soziologen in Baunatal: Facharbeiter, verheiratet, zwei Kinder, Neubauwohnung, Auto. Er ist und hat wohl alles, was in materieller Hinsicht als wünschenswert und erreichbar gilt. *1966*

Left:

The sociologist's ideal type for a resident of Baunatal: skilled tradesman, married, two children, modern flat, car. He is everything and probably has everything anyone could materially wish for. *1966*

Oben:

Keine Stadt ohne Badeanstalt. Im Bestreben, bei ihren Bürgern zu punkten, bauen die Kommunen wie in Essen großzügig alle möglichen Freizeiteinrichtungen. Einige Jahrzehnte später gehören diese zu den teuren Wohlstandsruinen. Die Menschen ziehen es vor, sich an den sonnigen Stränden des Südens zu erholen. *1963*

Above:

Every town has its public swimming baths. In their efforts to score points with their citizens, the local authorities generously build all kinds of leisure amenities, as here in Essen. A few decades later, they're among the costly white elephants of the affluent society. People prefer to seek recreation on the sunny beaches of the south. *1963*

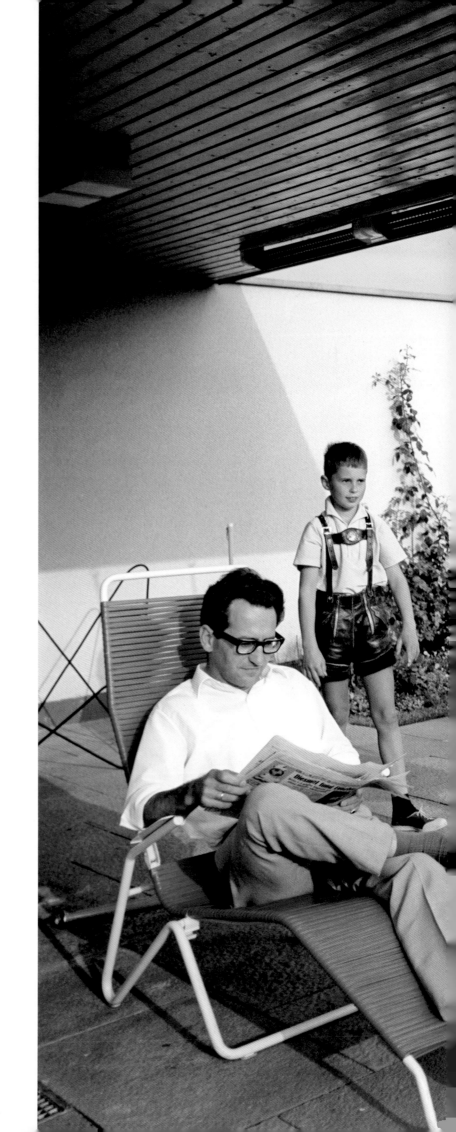

**Der besserverdienende deutsche Durchschnitts-
mensch:** Angestellter, verheiratet, drei Kinder, Reihen-
bungalow in der Neubausiedlung. *Frankfurt 1964*

The average German high earner: salaried employee,
married, three children, terraced bungalow on a newly-
built estate. *Frankfurt 1964*

Wirtschaft.
Die Schlote rauchen wieder

The Economy.
The factory chimneys are smoking again

Bis Mitte der 60er Jahre setzte sich der wirtschaftliche Aufschwung in der Bundesrepublik unvermindert fort. Das Bruttosozialprodukt glänzte mit nie wieder erreichten Steigerungsraten. Was man im In- und im Ausland einhellig als „Wirtschaftswunder" empfand, war für den verantwortlichen Bundesminister Ludwig Erhard nur das logische Resultat einer vernünftigen Wirtschaftspolitik. Orientiert an marktwirtschaftlichen Maßstäben, enthielt sie eine starke soziale Komponente. Die ständig brennende Zigarre des Politikers galt als symbolhaftes Zeichen für die freudige Kunde, dass die Schlote wieder rauchten. Obwohl eine stetig wachsende Zahl von Menschen vom zunehmenden Wohlstand profitierte, verbreiterte sich die Schere zwischen den gesellschaftlichen Schichten zusehends. Die Zweidrittelgesellschaft war vorgezeichnet. Als der Bundestag am 22. Januar 1957 dem Rentenreformgesetz, das die Lage der Rentner entscheidend verbesserte, seine Zustimmung gab, betrachtete Erhard den Beschluss als Sündenfall wider den Geist der Marktwirtschaft, ebenso wie die kontinuierliche Ausweitung des Sozialhaushalts. Der Wirtschaftsboom beschränkte sich nicht auf die Bundesrepublik, sondern erfasste die gesamte westliche Welt. Er war eine der Folgen des Koreakrieges mit der emporschießenden Nachfrage nach Produkten der Stahlindustrie. Außerdem hatte die deutsche Großindustrie durch den Bombenkrieg weniger gelitten, als die Trümmerwüsten ahnen ließen. Sie konnte schon zu Beginn der 50er Jahre an die alte Stärke anknüpfen. Der Export war der Transmissionsriemen des Wirtschaftswunders. Der Bedarf der Industrie an Arbeitskräften schnellte binnen kurzer Zeit hoch und trieb die Modernisierung des Landes rapide voran. Die Wirtschaft warb um die Frauen und heuerte die ersten „Gastarbeiter" aus Italien und der Türkei an. Außerdem vollzog sich in der Bundesrepublik binnen weniger Jahre ein tief greifender Strukturwandel. In der Landwirtschaft sank die Zahl der Beschäftigten von 23,2 % im Jahr 1950 auf 8,5 % im Jahr 1970. Die Bundesrepublik wandelte sich zur Industrie- und Dienstleistungsgesellschaft. Doch schon bald mussten die ersten Zechen stillgelegt werden, weil sie die Steinkohle nicht mehr rentabel zu fördern vermochten. Der technologische Vorsprung in anderen Branchen hielt die ökonomischen Konsequenzen in Grenzen. Dennoch endete die Phase des „Wirtschaftswunders" mit einer Rezession.

Until the mid-Sixties, economic recovery in the Federal Republic continued unabated. The gross national product turned in star performances with growth rates that have never been seen since. For Ludwig Erhard, the minister responsible, what was viewed unanimously at home and abroad as an "economic miracle" was just the logical consequence of a sensible economic policy. Based on the principles of a market economy, it had a strong social component. The politician's constantly lit cigar was seen as a symbol of the good news that the chimneys were smoking again. Although a steadily increasing number of people benefited from the growing prosperity, the divide between the social classes widened appreciably. The two-thirds society was becoming an inevitability. When the Bundestag approved the law on pension reform on 21 January 1957, considerably improving the lot of pensioners, Erhard saw the decision as a crime against the spirit of the market economy. Likewise the continual enlargement of the welfare budget. The economic boom was not restricted to the Federal Republic, but was experienced by the whole of the Western world. It was one of the consequences of the Korean War with the mushrooming demand for the products of the steel industry. Furthermore, Germany's major industry had suffered less through the bombing than the deserts of rubble had led people to believe. By the early Fifties, it was already performing to its old high standards. Exports were the driving force of the economic miracle. Industry's need for manpower escalated within a very short time and drove the modernization of the country rapidly forward. The economy made efforts to attract women and hired the first "immigrant workers" from Italy and Turkey. In addition, a far-reaching structural change took place within a few years in the Federal Republic. The number of people employed on the land fell from 23.2% in 1950 to 8.5% in 1970. The Federal Republic changed into an industrial and service society. But the first pits were already having to be closed because they were unable to mine coal cost-effectively. Technological advances in other branches of industry kept the economic consequences of this in check. Nevertheless the phase of the "economic miracle" ended with a recession.

Ein selbst gezimmertes Regal in der Kellergarage, und fertig ist der Laden. Die Eier sind immer frisch vom Land. 20 Pfennig kosten sie, kaum weniger als vierzig Jahre später. *Bonn 1955*

A home-made set of shelves in the garage under the house — and there's your shop. The eggs are always fresh from the country. They cost 20 pfennigs, scarcely any less than forty years later. *Bonn 1955*

Arbeiter mit der Teermaschine beim Ausbau einer Landstraße im Bayerischen Wald. Trotz der schwierigen Bedingungen und altertümlicher Arbeitsgeräte wächst das Straßennetz zwischen 1950 und 1960 um knapp 30.000 Kilometer. *1955*

Workers with tar-spreading machine extending a country road in the Bavarian Forest. Despite the difficult conditions and antiquated tools, the road network grows by 30,000 kilometres between 1950 and 1960. *1955*

Großmutter, Mutter und Tochter beim Distel-stechen auf einem Getreidefeld. Noch hat sich die Rationalisierung in der Landwirtschaft mit Maschinen und chemischen Hilfsmitteln nicht überall durchgesetzt. *1956*

Grandmother, mother and daughter hoeing thistles in a cornfield. Rationalization in farming with machinery and chemical expedients has not yet been adopted everywhere. *1956*

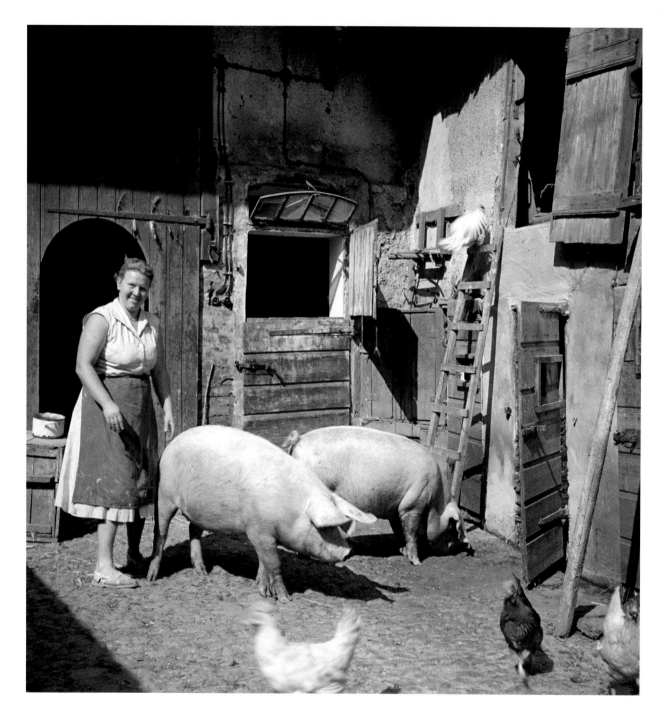

Oben:
Der Stolz der Bäuerin: das deutsche Hausschwein.
Hessen 1959

Above:
The farmer's wife's pride and joy: the German domestic pig. *Hesse 1959*

Rechts:
Getreideernte mit dem Mähdrescher. Die Zahl der Beschäftigten in der Landwirtschaft sinkt (von 25 % im Jahr 1950 auf 8 % im Jahr 1970), aber die Erträge steigen; auch in Niedersachsen bei Wilhelmshaven. *1959*

Right:
Getting in the corn with a combine harvester. The number of people employed in farming goes down (from 25% in 1950 to 8% in 1970), but there are increased returns; also in Lower Saxony near Wilhelmshaven. *1959*

Einige Bauern verkaufen ihre Produkte auf dem Markplatz in Cham neben einem Zeitungskiosk aus Brettern. Der kalte Herbstnebel drückt auf die ohnehin trübe Stimmung. *1955*

A handful of smallholders sell their products on Marktplatz in Cham next to a newspaper kiosk made of wooden boards. The chilly autumn mist adds to the already bleak atmosphere. *1955*

Das Geschäft kommt in Gang. Obst, Gemüse und andere Lebensmittel, die auf dem Marktplatz in Bonn angeboten werden, braucht schließlich jeder. Zudem trifft man hier Hinz und Kunz, und das ist das Schönste. *1953*

Business is getting going. Fruit, vegetables and other foodstuffs on offer in the market square in Bonn are things everyone needs, after all. And then of course you get to meet just about everyone you know, and that's the best thing of all. *1953*

Links:

Einkauf beim Kaufmann. Jeder Suppenwürfel wird einzeln begutachtet und über die Theke gereicht. Die Wartenden bilden Chor und Publikum zugleich. Man kennt sich, man trifft sich, man schwätzt miteinander. *Bonn 1956*

Left:

Shopping at the grocer's. Each stock cube is examined individually and passed over the counter. The people waiting are both the chorus and the audience. They know each other, are happy to meet and have a chat. *Bonn 1956*

Unten:

Vom Kasseler bis Kaviar ist alles wieder da, selbst Diätbrot für die Schonkostbedürftigen. Die Fresswelle rollt. 3.000 Kalorien täglich verdrücken die Deutschen im Schnitt. Delikatessengeschäft in Bonn. *1955*

Below:

From smoked pork to caviar — everything is available again. Even diet bread for those who have special nutritional needs. A wave of gluttony is on the move. On average the Germans polish off 3,000 calories a day. A delicatessen in Bonn. *1955*

Oben:
Setzerei im Druckhaus Deutz. Seit den Zeiten von Johannes Gutenberg war der Setzkasten das Herzstück jeder Druckerei. Jeder Buchstabe musste daraus einzeln entnommen werden. Maschinensatz und am Ende der Computer schickten ihn später ins Museum. *Köln 1955*

Above:
The composing room at Deutz Printworks. Since Johannes Gutenberg's day, the typecase had been at the centre of every printing works. Each letter had to be taken out of it individually. Machine setting and finally the computer relegated it to the museum. *Cologne 1955*

Rechts:
Fünf Drucker und eine Druckmaschine. In einer modernen Druckerei ist das Verhältnis umgekehrt. Druckhaus Deutz. *Köln 1955*

Right:
Five print workers to one printing press. In a modern printworks, it's the other way round. Deutz Printworks. *Cologne 1955*

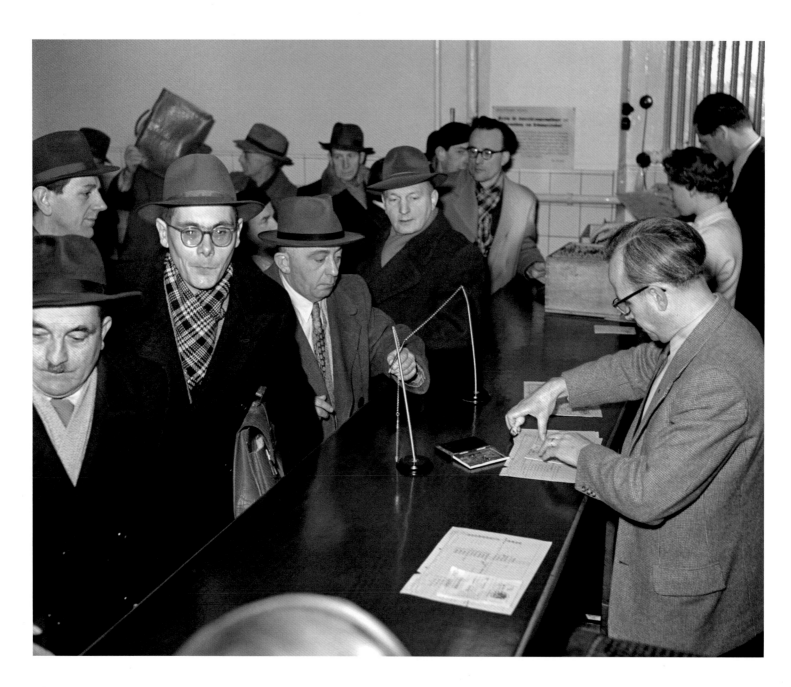

Oben:
Zahltag in Köln. Am Freitag wird der Lohn bar aus-
gezahlt. Der Beleg besteht aus einem schmalen Streifen
Papier. Ein Bankkonto unterhalten nur die
„Bessergestellten". *1956*

Above:
Payday in Cologne. Wages are paid out in cash on
Fridays. The pay slip is a narrow strip of paper. Only the
"better off" have a bank account. *1956*

Rechts:
Montage von Musikboxen in Espelkamp. Man erkennt
den Arm, der mit geheimnisvoller Präzision die ge-
wünschte Platte herausfischt und sanft auf dem Teller
niederlegt. *1957*

Right:
Assembling juke boxes in Espelkamp. It's possible to
make out the arm that selects the chosen record with
mysterious precision and lays it gently on the turntable.
1957

Hochofenabstich in der Eisenhütte Neunkirchen,
Saarland. *1960*

**Tapping the blast furnace at the ironworks in
Neunkirchen,** Saarland. *1960*

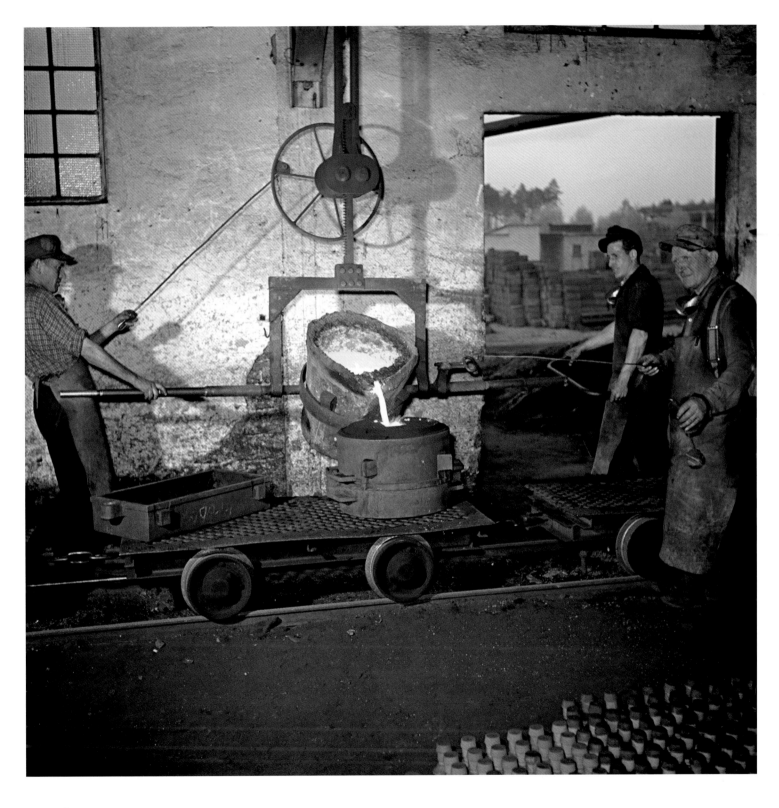

Eisengießerei in Hessen. *1955*

Iron foundry in Hesse. *1955*

In einer kleinen Halle des Stuttgarter Werkes schrauben die Monteure Porsche-Flitzer vom Typ 356 zusammen. Deren Luxus hält sich in Grenzen. Ein Porsche kostet dennoch rund 18.000 DM, dreimal so viel wie ein VW-Käfer vom Typ Export. *1957*

In a small shed at the works in Stuttgart, mechanics assemble Porsche 356 sports cars. The degree of luxury is quite limited. Nevertheless a Porsche costs 18,000 marks, three times as much as a VW Beetle Export. *1957*

Leukoplast-Bomber heißt der Lloyd LP 400 im Volksmund, denn die Karosserie besteht aus Sperrholz und Kunstleder, erst später aus Stahl und Blech. 12 PS aus einem 400-Kubikzentimeter-Motor treiben den Zweitakter an. Seine Fahrleistungen sind bescheiden. Aber er sorgt für Mobilität bei kleinen Ansprüchen. Ab 1950 baut die Firma Borgward in Bremen den Kleinwagen. *1955*

Sticking plaster bomber is what people jokingly call the Lloyd LP 400 because the bodywork is plywood and imitation leather, only later replaced by steel and sheet metal. 12 HP from a 400 cc. engine power the two-stroker. Its road performance is modest. But it provides mobility for people on a low budget. Borgward started building this small car in 1950 in Bremen. *1955*

Oben:

Auf dem Bundeskanzlerplatz in Bonn regelt bei Bedarf ein Polizist „op de Tonn" (auf der Tonne) den Verkehr. Kein Vergleich mit dem Verkehrsgewühl in den anderen europäischen Hauptstädten. *1960*

Rechts:

Kleeblatt. Beim Blick aus der Luft springt der Name für das Frankfurter Kreuz förmlich ins Auge. Die anschwellenden Verkehrsströme, für die es konzipiert ist, lassen nicht auf sich warten. *1957*

Above:

On the Bundeskanzlerplatz in Bonn, a policeman "on the barrel" controls the traffic when necessary. No comparison with the traffic chaos in the other European capitals. *1960*

Right:

Clover leaf. Seen from the air, it's obvious where the Frankfurt motorway interchange gets its name. The increasing volumes of traffic it was designed to deal with arc not long coming. *1957*

Seite 126/127:

Die Zahl der Autos auf den Straßen wächst rapide.
Waren es 1950 eine halbe Million, sind es 1960 bereits
3,7 Millionen Autos und 1970 gar 13,5 Millionen. In
gleichem Tempo steigt die Zahl der Unfälle – mit und
ohne tödliche Folgen. „Freie Fahrt für freie Bürger" heißt
die Losung auf den Autobahnen. Wegen der sich häufen-
den Frontalzusammenstöße errichtet man alsbald Leit-
planken zwischen den Fahrbahnen. Ein tödlicher Unfall
bei Karlsruhe. *1964*

Page 126/127:

The numbers of cars on the roads increases rapidly.
Half a million in 1950, then 3.7 million in 1960 and an
amazing 13.5 million in 1970. The number of accidents
rises in proportion – with and without fatalities. "Free
driving for free citizens" is the motto on the motorways.
In response to the mounting frequency of head-on
collisions, crash barriers are soon installed between the
carriageways. A fatal accident near Karlsruhe. *1964*

Links:

**Die Glaspaläste der Industrieverwaltungen entlang
der Stadtautobahn in Duisburg,** ein bisher in
Deutschland unbekanntes urbanes Ensemble. *1962*

Left:

**The glass palaces of industry's office buildings along
the urban motorway in Duisburg,** a hitherto unknown
urban ensemble. *1962*

Unten:

**Hauptwache, ein Platz in Frankfurt, und der Kaufhof,
alles unter einem Dach.** Die Innenstadt fiel fast ganz
den Bomben zum Opfer. Im funktionellen Stil der
Moderne wird sie wieder aufgebaut: schnell und manchmal, aber nicht immer, ästhetisch anspruchslos. *1957*

Below:

**Hauptwache, a square in Frankfurt, and the Kaufhof
department store with everything under one roof.**
The city centre was almost totally destroyed in the
bombing. It is rebuilt in the functional modernist style,
fast and sometimes, though not always, aesthetically
uninspiring. *1957*

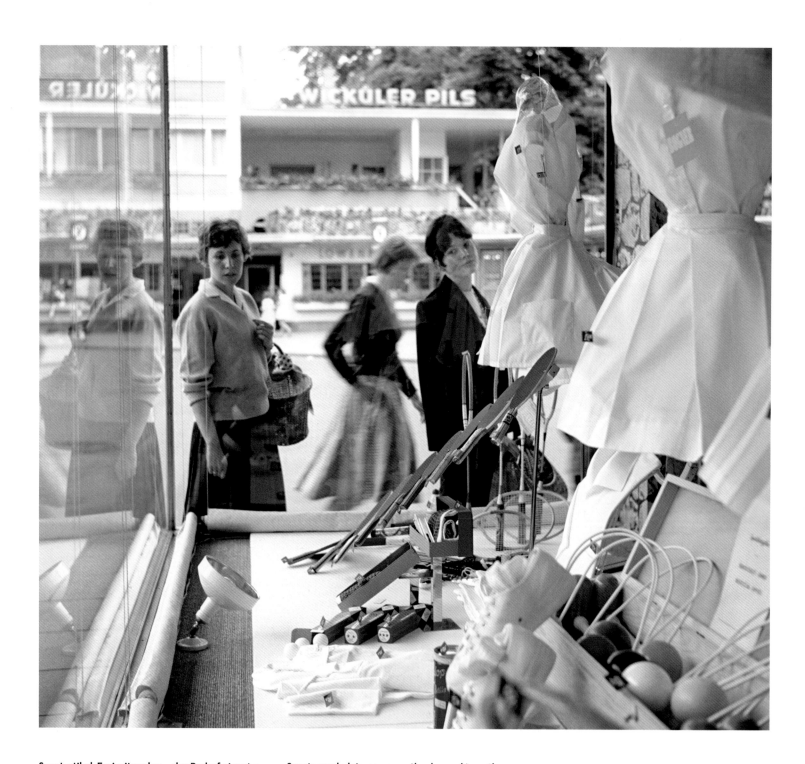

Sportartikel, Freizeitmoden — der Bedarf nimmt zu.
Die Mode signalisiert das Anwachsen der Freizeit im
Leben der Menschen, das Angebot für den Freizeitsport
ein verstärktes Körperbewusstsein. Das Ladengeschäft in
Bad Godesberg. *1962*

**Sports goods, leisurewear — the demand is on the
increase.** Fashion is an indicator of increasing free time
in people's lives. The range of leisure sports reflects a
heightened body awareness. A shop in Bad Godesberg.
1962

Schaufenster eines Geschäftes für Damenmode in Frankfurt. Die pompös gerahmte Landidylle im Hintergrund ist pure Dekoration und hat keinen Bezug zu den zelebrierten Modellen. *1964*

Window display of a ladieswear boutique in Frankfurt. The ostentatiously framed painting of a rural scene in the background is just decoration and has no relevance to the models paraded here. *1964*

Links:
Das Warenhaus Kaufhof bietet beim Sommer-schlussverkauf seine modischen Güter zu Schleuder-preisen an. Nach der Öffnung am Montagmorgen werden unter den Schnäppchenjägerinnen regelrechte Kampfszenen beobachtet. *Frankfurt 1958*

Left:
The Kaufhof department store slashes the prices of its fashionable wares in the summer sales. When they opened on Monday morning, it came to fisticuffs among some of the bargain hunters. *Frankfurt 1958*

Oben:
Kaufen, was die Taschen fassen – Schlussverkauf im Frankfurter Kaufhof. *1958*

Above:
Grab as much as you can carry – the sales at Frankfurt's Kaufhof. *1958*

Links:
Steno und Schreibmaschine heißen die Fertigkeiten, die eine Tür zur begehrten Arbeit im Büro öffnen. Doch höher hinauf als bis zur Chefsekretärin führt die Karriereleiter nur selten. Schreibmaschinenunterricht in der Berufsschule von Groß-Gerau. *1959*

Left:
Shorthand typing is the skill that will open the door to a sought-after office job. But the career ladder rarely leads to anything higher than personal assistant. Learning typing at the vocational school in Groß-Gerau. *1959*

Oben:
Deutsch für Ausländer in Heidelberg. Die deutschen Universitäten haben einen guten Ruf, die Stipendien auch. Die Deutschen geben sich weltoffen. Sie haben etwas gutzumachen. *1962*

Above:
German for foreigners in Heidelberg. German universities have a good reputation, as do the bursaries they offer. The Germans are anxious to appear cosmopolitan. They have something to make good. *1962*

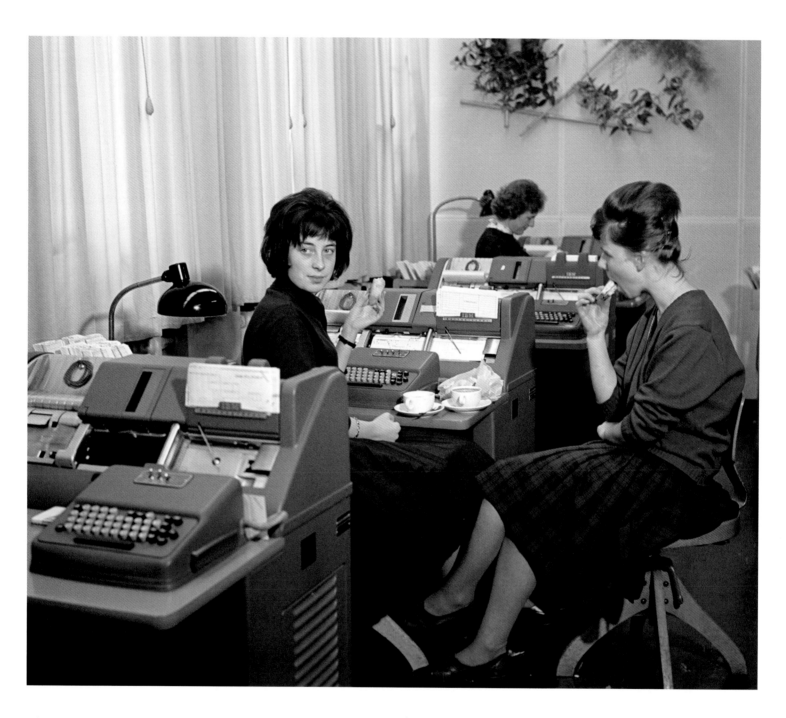

Oben:
Frühstückspause. Zwischen den Lochkartenmaschinen essen die Angestellten ihr mitgebrachtes Pausenbrot. *Fürth 1958*

Above:
Morning break. The filing clerks eat their sandwiches among the punch-card machines. *Fürth 1958*

Rechts:
Das Versandhaus Quelle in Fürth nutzt als erstes Unternehmen die Möglichkeiten der elektronischen Datenverarbeitung: IBM Computer Typ 701. Das System funktioniert schnell und zuverlässig – und spart rare Arbeitskräfte. *1958*

Right:
The mail-order business Quelle in Fürth is the first company to exploit the possibilities of electronic data processing: IBM Computer Type 701. The system is fast and reliable – and cuts down on scarce manpower. *1958*

136

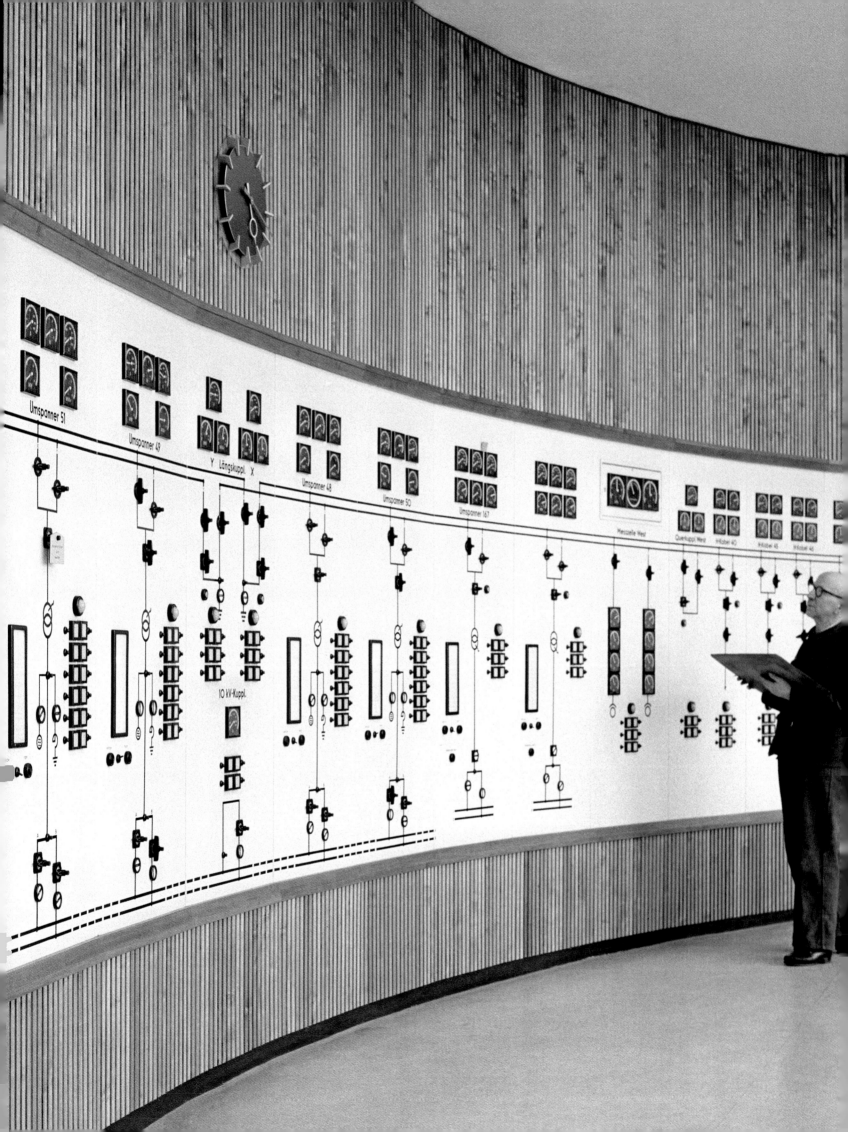

Links:
Wer denkt, wer lenkt? Eine Schalttafel im Elektrizitäts-
werk von Frankfurt am Main. Die Automatisierung
schreitet unaufhaltsam voran. *1964*

Left:
Who decides what here? A control panel in the
electricity works in Frankfurt/Main. The advance of
automation is unstoppable. *1964*

Unten:
Mit modernster Anlagentechnik kontrollieren nur zwei
Arbeiter eine gewaltige Maschinerie in den Chemischen
Werken Hüls in Marl. *1960*

Below:
State-of-the-art technical systems allow just two
workers to monitor a vast amount of machinery in the
Hüls Chemical Works in Marl. *1960*

Links:
In der Nacht verbreiteten die Stahlöfen ein gespenstisches Licht um die Völklinger Hütte, in der Eisenerz aus dem benachbarten Lothringen verarbeitet wurde. *Saarland 1960*

Left:
At night the steel furnaces cast an eerie light around the Völklinger steelworks, where iron ore from neighbouring Lorraine was processed. *Saarland 1960*

Unten:
Industrielandschaft an der Saar.
Völklingen 1960

Below:
Industrial landscape on the Saar.
Völklingen 1960

Unten:
Roter Himmel über dem Ruhrgebiet am Rhein bei Duisburg. Nur wenige Sonnenstrahlen dringen durch den Schleier aus Abgasen und Staub, Atembeschwerden nehmen zu. Die Politik nimmt den blauen Himmel ins Angebot, die Industrie verweist auf die Kosten. *1959*

Below:
A red sky over the Ruhr on the Rhine near Duisburg. The sun's rays can hardly penetrate the veil of exhaust fumes and dust. Respiratory complaints are on the increase. Politics embraces the ambition of a blue sky; industry points out the costs. *1959*

Rechts:
Bei der Stahlgewinnung stieg in regelmäßigen Abständen eine schrecklich-schöne Abgaswolke über dem Thyssen-Stahlwerk in Duisburg auf. Als Ministerpräsident Fritz Steinhoff im Landtagswahlkampf den blauen Himmel über der Ruhr versprach, lachten die meisten. Seitdem viel Stahl aus Asien kommt und aktiver Umweltschutz zur gesellschaftlichen Forderung wurde, ist die Luft besser. *1958*

Right:
Steel production put out horrendous, if beautiful clouds of waste gas at regular intervals over the Thyssen Steelworks in Duisburg. When prime minister Fritz Steinhoff promised blue skies over the Ruhr in the election campaign for the regional parliament, most people just laughed. When a lot of steel began to be imported from Asia, and society started demanding pollution control, the air improved. *1958*

Schiffslände in Deutz.
Köln 1960

Below:
Shipping wharf in Deutz.
Cologne 1960

Rechts:
Stülcken-Werft, Hamburg. Bewährte Qualität zu einem vernünftigen Preis ist das Erfolgsrezept des deutschen Schiffbaus. Bald löst die preiswertere Konkurrenz aus Asien eine landesweite Werftenkrise aus. Der deutsche Schiffbau antwortet nach einem lang anhaltenden Niedergang erfolgreich mit Spezialisierung. *1960*

Right:
Stülcken Wharf, Hamburg. Proven quality at a reasonable price is German shipbuilding's recipe for success. Cheaper competition from Asia soon triggers an all-embracing shipyard crisis. After a long downturn, specialization proves the right answer for Germany's shipbuilders. *1960*

Politik.
Auf nach Westen

Politics.
Let's go West!

Der satte Stimmengewinn seiner Partei im Wahlkampf 1953 bestätigte Konrad Adenauers planmäßig betriebene Politik einer festen Einbindung der Bundesrepublik Deutschland in die westliche Hemisphäre. Nur knapp verfehlte er die absolute Mehrheit. Deutschland war geteilt, und an der Demarkationslinie zwischen Ost und West standen sich zwei hochgerüstete Militärblöcke unversöhnlich gegenüber. Die wechselseitige Drohung, den jeweils anderen mit Atomwaffen zu vernichten, sicherte dank einer Art „Gleichgewicht des Schreckens" die bestehenden Machtverhältnisse – im Westen unter Führung der USA, im Osten der UdSSR. Immer wieder eskalierte der Konflikt um Westberlin, die „Insel der freien Welt" inmitten der sowjetischen Einflusssphäre. Vor der Folie eines unverminderten wirtschaftlichen Aufschwungs erhielt die Politik der konsequenten Eingliederung in das politische, wirtschaftliche und kulturelle Gefüge des Westens während der folgenden Jahre eine neue Qualität – auch um den Preis, dass sich die Teilung des Landes zunächst vertiefte. Systematischer Ausbau der bereits bestehenden europäischen Institutionen und der Beitritt zum westlichen Bündnis der NATO pflasterten den Weg in eine unumkehrbare Richtung. Der wichtigste Schritt war die Aussöhnung mit Frankreich. 1959 bekannte sich auch die größte Oppositionspartei im Bundestag, die SPD, zu den Grundsätzen dieser Politik. Der Bau der Mauer im August 1961 schien für kurze Zeit die Gefahr eines Dritten Weltkrieges heraufzubeschwören. Tatsächlich förderte die Mauer die Konsolidierung und bedeutete zugleich den definitiven Abschied des Sowjetkommunismus von seinen Expansionsbestrebungen in Europa. Die 1960er-Jahre waren eine Zeit des allmählichen Übergangs und der mentalen Veränderung. Ihre zweite Hälfte stand im Zeichen einer Großen Koalition der beiden führenden Parteien sowie einer Politik vorsichtiger Annäherung an den Osten und der Studentenrevolte im Inneren.

The greatly increased share of the vote for his party in the elections of 1953 was an endorsement of Konrad Adenauer's systematically pursued policy of firmly integrating the Federal Republic of Germany into the western hemisphere. He only just missed winning an absolute majority. Germany was divided, and on the demarcation line between East and West, two military blocs faced each other, implacable and armed to the teeth. Thanks to a kind of "balance of terror", the reciprocal threat that one would destroy the other by the use of nuclear weapons safeguarded the existing balance of power: in the West under the leadership of the USA, and in the East under that of the USSR. The conflict escalated continually over West Berlin, the "island of the free world" in the middle of the Soviet sphere of influence. Against the backdrop of an unabated economic recovery, the policy of moving consistently towards integration into the political, economic and cultural fabric of the West took on a new quality during the following years – even at the price of initially deepening the divide between the two parts of the country. The systematic expansion of the existing European institutions and the entry into the western alliance of NATO led in a direction from which there was no way back. The most important step was the reconciliation with France. In 1959 the largest opposition party in the Bundestag, the SPD, declared its support for the principles of this policy. The building of the Wall in August 1961 looked briefly as though it was in danger of provoking a third world war. In fact, it expedited consolidation and at the same time meant a definitive end to the expansionist ambitions of Soviet Communism in Europe. The Sixties were a time of gradual transition and a change of mindset. The second half of the decade was played out against the background of a grand coalition of the two leading parties, of a policy, in foreign affairs, of cautious rapprochement with the East, and of student unrest on the domestic front.

Eins, zwei, drei, vier, Marsch mit Fahne und Gesang – Wandervogel-Romantik der dreißiger Jahre erfüllte die organisierte Parteijugend auch nach dem Desaster von Diktatur und Krieg. Beim sozialistischen Jugendtag in Dortmund. *1955*

One, two, three, four. Marching with flag and song – the romanticism of the Wandervogel youth movement of the Thirties remained an attraction for the young members of political parties, even after the disaster of dictatorship and war. At the Young Socialists' Convention in Dortmund. *1955*

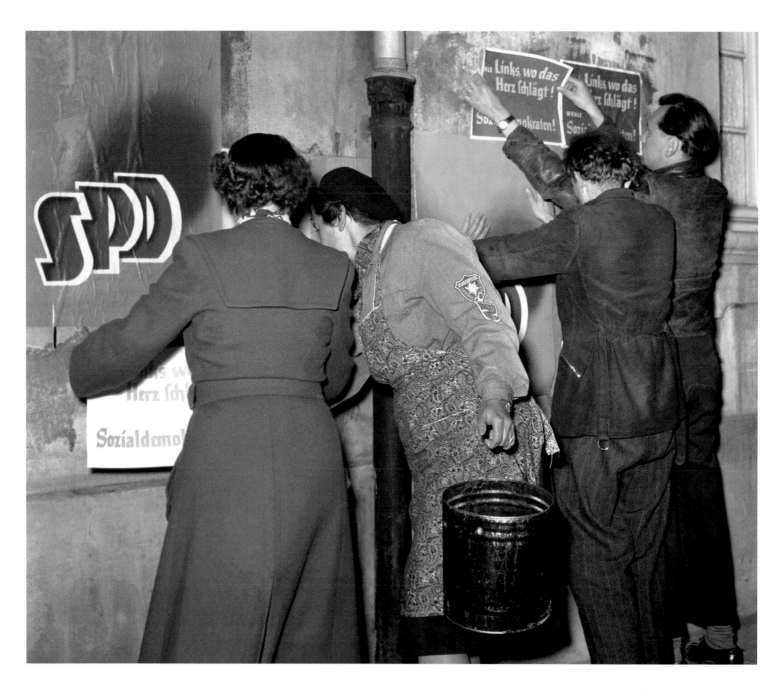

Links schlägt das Herz, aber rechts sitzt die Brief-tasche. Nach diesem Motto wird sich das Wahlvolk ent-scheiden. CDU und CSU verfehlen unter Führung von Bundeskanzler Konrad Adenauer nur knapp die absolute Mehrheit. Plakatkleben im Bundestagswahlkampf. *Bonn 1953*

The heart beats on the left, but the right is where the wallet is. This is what will influence the voters. Under the leadership of Konrad Adenauer, CDU and CSU narrowly miss winning an absolute majority. Putting up posters in the federal election campaign. *Bonn 1953*

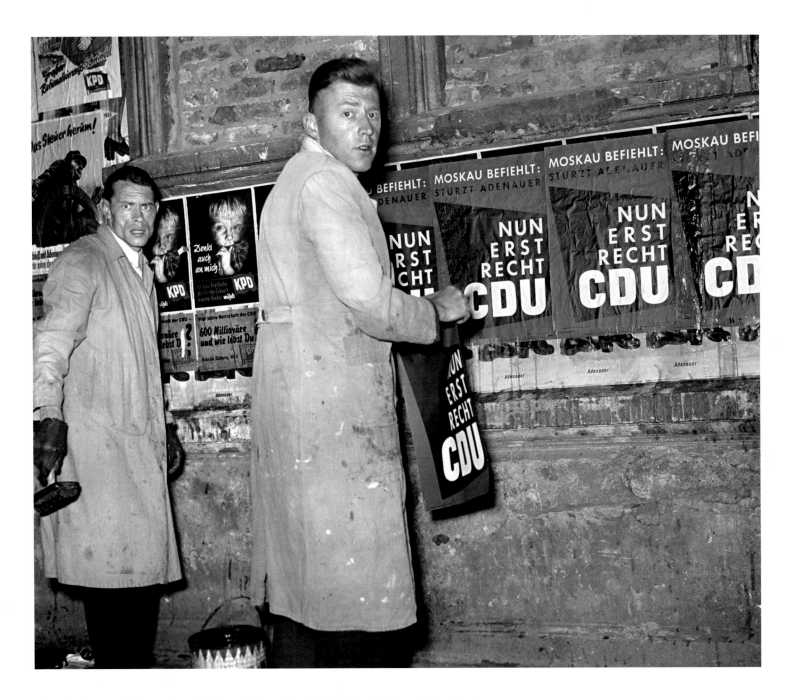

Ob sie dürfen, was sie da tun, wissen die Herrschaften offenbar nicht so genau. Deshalb funktioniert es nachts auch besser. Ein Trupp fürs Plakatkleben im Bundestagswahlkampf. Der Fotograf hat ihn in Bonn gestellt. *1953*

They clearly don't really know whether they're allowed to do what they're doing. So better do it at night. A gang of bill stickers during the federal election campaign. The photographer caught them at it in Bonn. *1953*

Seite 150/151:

15 Parteien werben mit ihren Plakaten vor der Abstimmung im französischen Protektoratsgebiet, das Frankreich nach dem Krieg in sein Wirtschaftsterritorium eingegliedert hatte: Soll das Saarland zu Deutschland kommen oder europäisiert werden? 67 % der Bewohner lehnen das Saarstatut ab und ermöglichen damit den erneuten Anschluss des Saarlandes an die Bundesrepublik. *Saarbrücken 1955*

Page 150/151:

15 parties canvas with their posters before the referendum in the French protectorate, which France had incorporated into its economic territory. Should Saarland come back to Germany or become Europeanized? 67.7% of Saarlanders vote against the Saarstatut, paving the way for Saarland to join the Federal Republic. *Saarbrücken 1955*

Links und unten:

Der Landweg nach Berlin über die Transit-autobahnen ist mit Plakaten der DDR-Propaganda gepflastert. Diese günstige Gelegenheit zur Einflussnahme lässt sie sich nicht entgehen. Keiner kann ihr ausweichen. Da aber die Menschen die konkurrierenden Systeme vor allem nach ihrem persönlichen Wohlergehen beurteilen, bleibt die Mühe vergeblich. Hier im Visier: die westdeutsche Wiederbewaffnung. *1956*

Left and below:

The overland route to Berlin via the transit motorway is plastered with GDR propaganda posters. This easy opportunity to exert influence is too tempting. There is no way around it. But since people judge the competing systems by their personal well-being, it's a vain endeavour. This time the target is West German rearmament. *1956*

Wahlplakate. Alle wollen das Gleiche, nämlich dasselbe wie bisher. Wie soll es weitergehen? Genau so. Die Wähler gingen trotzdem zur Wahl, und die CDU erreichte als erste (und bisher einzige) Partei in der Geschichte der Bundesrepublik bei einer Bundestagswahl mit 50,2 % der abgegebenen Stimmen die absolute Mehrheit. *Bonn 1957*

Below:
Election posters. "No experiments" (CDU); "Enough experiments" (SPD). Everyone wants the same – the same as before. How should things continue? – Just as they were. The voters went to the polls nonetheless, and the CDU became the first (and to date only) party in the history of the federal republic to win an absolute majority at the federal elections with 50.2% of the ballots cast. *Bonn 1957*

Rechts:
Bisher war der Samstag ein Arbeitstag. Die Gewerkschaften setzten gegen starke Widerstände die Fünftagewoche mit 40 Arbeitsstunden durch. „Samstags gehört Vati mir", plakatierten sie das unterstellte Verlangen der Familien. Am 25. Juli 1955 hatten sich IG Metall und Arbeitgeber im „Bremer Abkommen" erstmals in einem Tarifgebiet auf die Fünftagewoche geeinigt. *1957*

Right:
Until now, Saturday had been a working day. Against vigorous opposition, the trades unions forced through their demand for a forty-hour, five-day week. "On Saturday, Daddy belongs to me" was the message of their poster campaign for what, they implied, the family wants. On 25 July 1955, in the so-called "Bremen Accord", the trade union IG Metall and the employers had agreed the five-day week for the first time in a tariff area. *1957*

Bergarbeiter tragen bei einer Demonstration in Dortmund die Bilder von Bundeskanzler Adenauer und Wirtschaftsminister Erhard wie Ikonen vor sich her. Den Niedergang des Steinkohlebergbaus können die beiden nicht aufhalten. Importkohle, Öl und Gas sind billiger als die deutsche Steinkohle. Heftige soziale Konflikte kennzeichnen die fünfziger Jahre. *1959*

At a demonstration in Dortmund, miners carry portraits of Federal Chancellor Adenauer and economics minister Erhard. The two of them can do nothing to stop the decline of the coalmining industry. Imported coal, oil and gas are cheaper than German coal. Bitter social conflicts are typical of the Fifties, too. *1959*

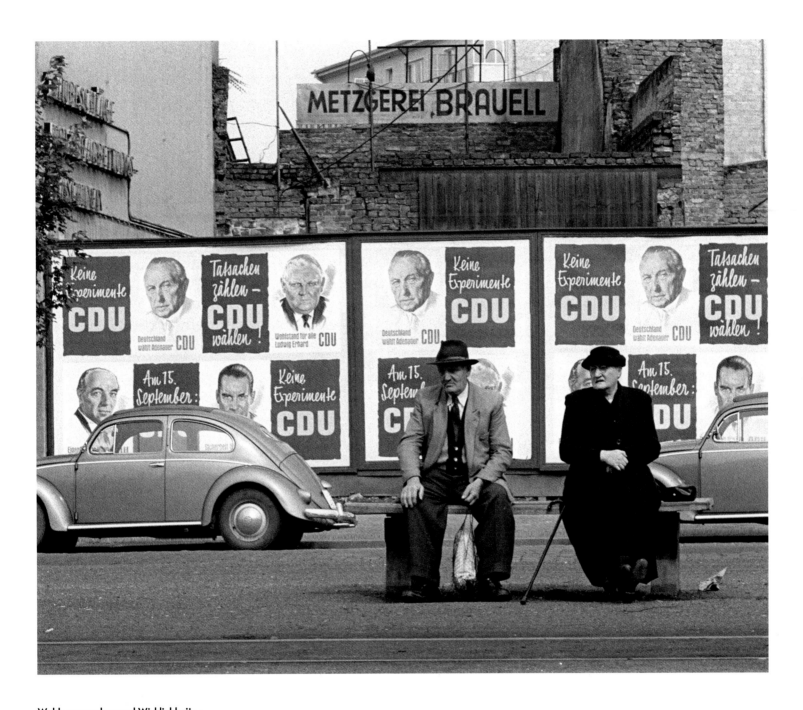

Wahlversprechen und Wirklichkeit —
Bundestagswahlkampf. *1957*

Election promises and the real world —
federal election campaign. *1957*

Unten:

Vierzig Jahre lang verharrt die Welt im latenten Kriegszustand zwischen West und Ost, NATO auf der einen, Warschauer Pakt auf der anderen Seite, bis an die Zähne bewaffnet. Als „Gleichgewicht des Schreckens" apostrophieren maßgebliche Politiker die prekäre Situation. Doch trotz mancher Ausschläge der Waage sichert das fragile „Patt" den Frieden in Europa. *Bonn 1959*

Below:

For forty years the world remains in a latent state of war between West and East, with NATO on one side and the Warsaw Pact on the other, both armed to the teeth. Leading politicians apostrophize the precarious situation as a "balance of terror". But despite a number of violent swings of the pointer, the fragile "stalemate" secures the fragile peace in Europe. *Bonn 1959*

Rechts:

„Nie wieder" — das war der Wille der meisten Deutschen. Adenauer ließ am 1. März 1956 die ersten Rekruten der Bundeswehr in Andernach, unweit von Bonn, strammstehen. Nur zur Landesverteidigung: versprochen – für alle Zeiten. *1956*

Right:

"Never again" — that was the way most Germans wanted it. On 1 March 1956, Adenauer had the first recruits to the Federal Armed Forces stand at attention in Andernach not far from Bonn. Only for the defence of the realm: a pledge – for all time. *1956*

Links:
Papa Heuss fährt vor. Den ersten deutschen Bundespräsidenten hielt die Kälte nicht davon ab, sich im offenen Wagen den Menschen als freundlicher Übervater zu
zeigen. Theodor Heuss hatte – anders als Kanzler
Adenauer – die Gabe, mit jovialem Gestus Versöhnlich-
keit und Zuversicht zu verbreiten. Auch in Bergneustadt.
Das trug ihm große Popularität und seinen liebevollen
Spitznamen ein. *1956*

Left:
Papa Heuss arrives. Using an open car despite the cold,
the first Federal President of Germany presents himself
to people as a friendly father figure. Unlike Chancellor
Adenauer, Theodor Heuss had an air of joviality about
him which inspired conciliatoriness and confidence. In
Bergneustadt, too. It earned him great popularity – and
his affectionate nickname. *1956*

Oben:
**Vor dem Bundeshaus in Bonn steigt ein Minister in
seinen Wagen.** Das Publikum ist nicht sonderlich beein-
druckt. *1958*

Above:
**Outside the federal parliament building a minister
gets into his car.** The public are not overly impressed.
1958

161

Hinweisschild bei der Grenzübergangsstelle Dreilinden an der Autobahn von Hannover kurz vor Westberlin: „Bis West-Berlin erneut 3 km durch Sowjetische Zone". *1958*

Sign at the Dreilinden border crossing point on the motorway from Hanover just before West Berlin: "To West Berlin another 3 km through the Soviet zone". *1958*

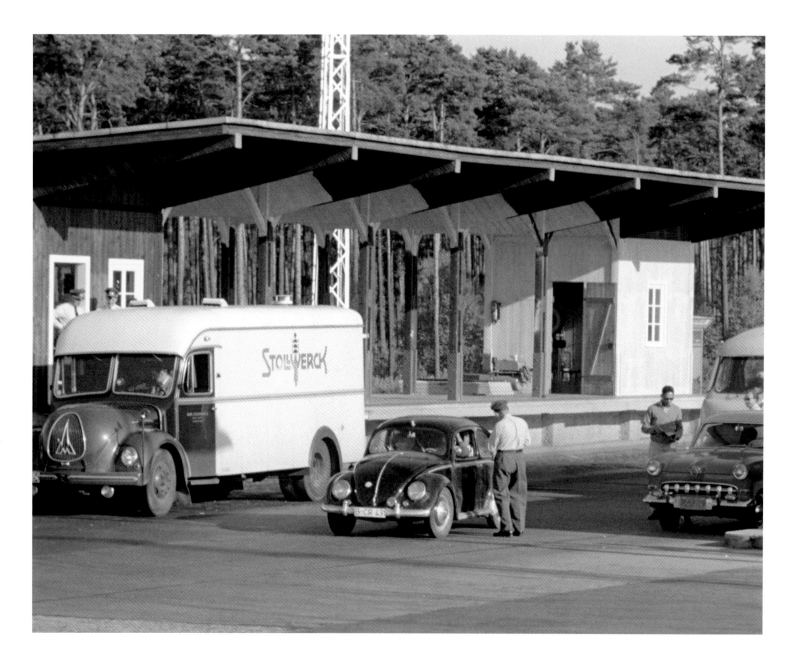

Kontrollstelle Marienborn. Jeder Lastwagen, auch im Transit nach Westberlin, wird durchsucht. Das ist nicht nur Schikane. Die Grenzsoldaten suchen auch „Republikflüchtige". 1956 verlassen 279.189 Menschen die DDR. *1956*

Checkpoint Marienborn. Every lorry is searched, even those in transit to West Berlin. It isn't just harassment. The border guards are also looking for so-called "absconders from the Republic". In 1956, 279,189 people leave the GDR. *1956*

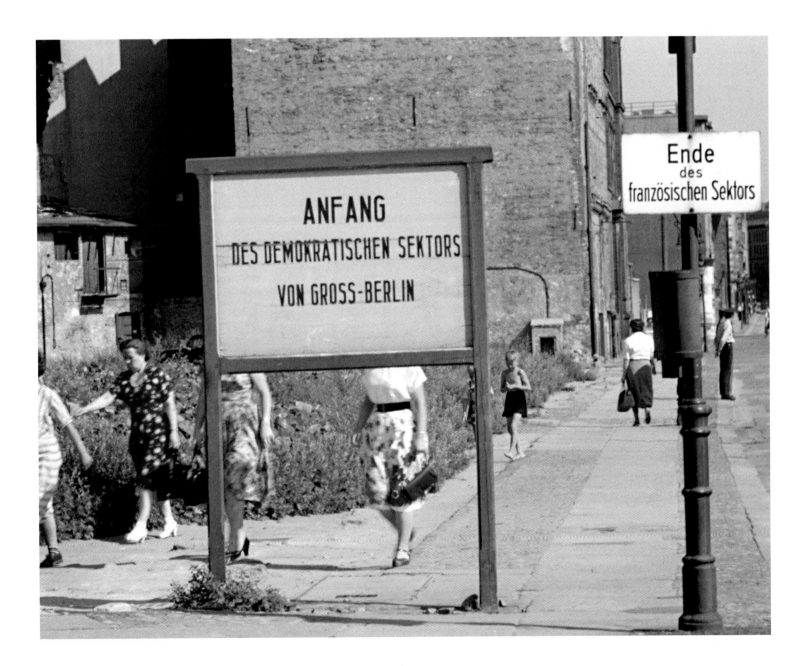

Noch ist die Grenze zwischen Ost und West an der Bernauer Straße in Berlin allein durch Schilder markiert. Die Menschen können sie ungehindert passieren. Die Volkspolizisten im Hintergrund scheinen sich nicht um sie zu kümmern. Der sowjetisch besetzte Teil der Stadt firmiert propagandistisch als „demokratischer Sektor". Bald schon werden Wachhäuschen das friedliche Bild stören. *1956*

The border between east and west along the Bernauer Straße in Berlin is still marked just by signs. People can cross over without being stopped. The people's police in the background don't seem to be taking any notice. The Soviet-occupied part of the city operates propagandistically under the name of "Democratic Sector". Guard posts will soon spoil the peaceful picture. *1956*

Links:

Auf dem Uhrenturm funkelt der Sowjetstern nach Westen. Die immer gleichen schalen Propagandaparolen trüben seine Ausstrahlung. Lederfabrik Hirschberg in der DDR. *1962*

Left:

The Soviet star on the clock tower twinkles towards the west. The same old vapid propaganda slogans rather tarnish its shine. The Hirschberg leather factory in the GDR. *1962*

Unten:

Die Sektorengrenze zwischen West und Ost an der Stresemannstraße in Berlin ist durch hölzerne Sperrgitter markiert und ansonsten offen. Viele nutzen dies, um die versprochene glückliche Zukunft im Sozialismus hinter sich zu lassen. *1959*

Below:

The sector border between West and East on Stresemannstraße in Berlin is marked by wooden barriers but is otherwise open. A lot of people take advantage of this to turn their backs on the promise of a happy future in socialism. *1959*

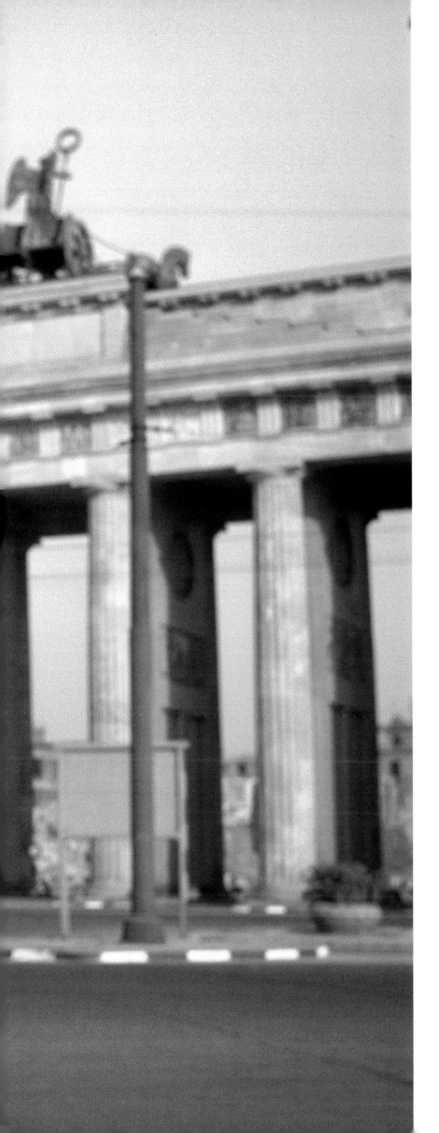

Willy Brandt vor dem Brandenburger Tor. Ein Jahr zuvor ist der politische Emigrant und Präsident des Berliner Abgeordnetenhauses zum Regierenden Bürgermeister von Berlin gewählt worden. 1961 wird er als Kanzlerkandidat der SPD gegen Bundeskanzler Konrad Adenauer antreten. *1958*

Willy Brandt in front of the Brandenburg Gate. A year earlier, the political émigré and president of Berlin's House of Representatives was elected governing mayor of Berlin. In 1961, as the SPD's candidate for the office of Chancellor, he will run against Federal Chancellor Konrad Adenauer. *1958*

171

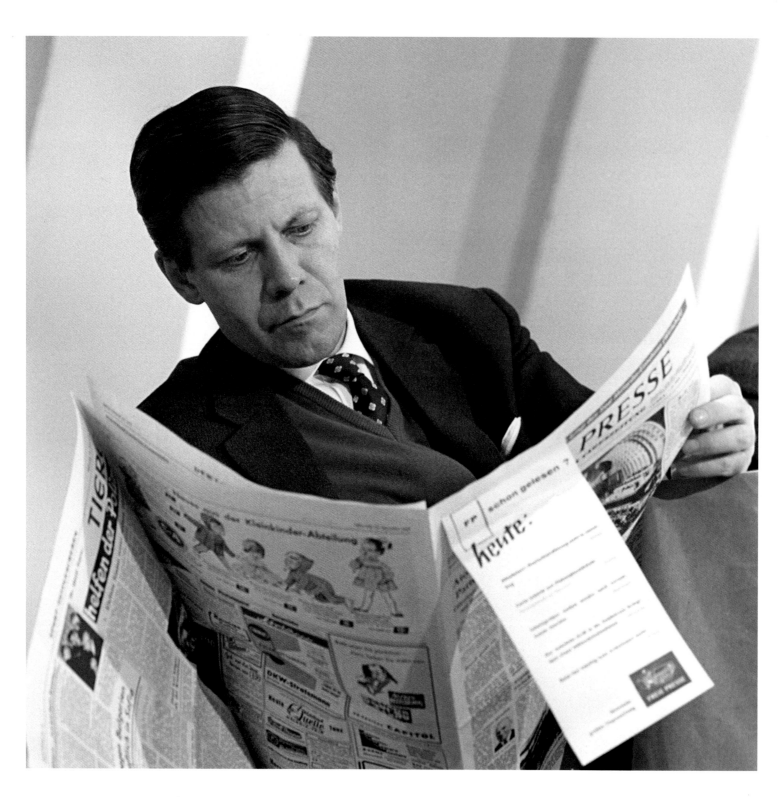

Oben:
Helmut Schmidt, ein junger Mann mit großer Zukunft. Als Bundestagsabgeordneter hatte sich der brillante Debattenredner den Spitznamen „Schmidt Schnauze" verdient. Die Bewährung als Krisenmanager und Innensenator Hamburgs bei der großen Sturmflut im Februar 1962 steht ihm noch bevor. *Hannover 1961*

Above:
Helmut Schmidt, a young man with a big future. As a member of parliament, he had earned the nickname of "Schmidt Big Mouth" for his brilliant debating skills. The testing time, as crisis manager and Interior Minister for the city-state of Hamburg during the great storm tide in February 1962, is still ahead of him. *Hanover 1961*

Rechts:
Willy Brandt, Kanzlerkandidat der SPD, tourt als Herausforderer von Konrad Adenauer durch die Bundesrepublik. Selbst ein Rheindampfer, hier bei der Abfahrt aus Bacharach, verwandelt sich in eine politische Plattform. *1961*

Right:
Willy Brandt, SPD Chancellor candidate, tours the Federal Republic as the challenger of Konrad Adenauer. Even a Rhine steamer, seen here leaving Bacharach, is transformed into a political platform. *1961*

Die Stalinallee in Ostberlin, die sozialistische Prunk- und Prachtstraße mit großzügigen Wohnungen, trotz schwieriger wirtschaftlicher Verhältnisse. Auch geeignet, um Waffenparaden im Stechschritt zu veranstalten. Das ästhetische Gegenbild ist der Kurfürstendamm in West- berlin. Eher vom Geldbeutel als von der Neuen Beschei- denheit diktiert, beherrscht nüchterne schnörkellose Strenge das „Schaufenster des Westens". *1959*

Stalinallee in East Berlin, the socialist show boulevard with splendid homes despite difficult economic circum- stances. Also suitable for staging weapons parades with goose-step. The aesthetic counter-image is the Kur- fürstendamm in West Berlin. Dictated by the purse rather than the New Unpretentiousness, the main note in the "shop window of the West" is a sober, no-frills austerity. *1959*

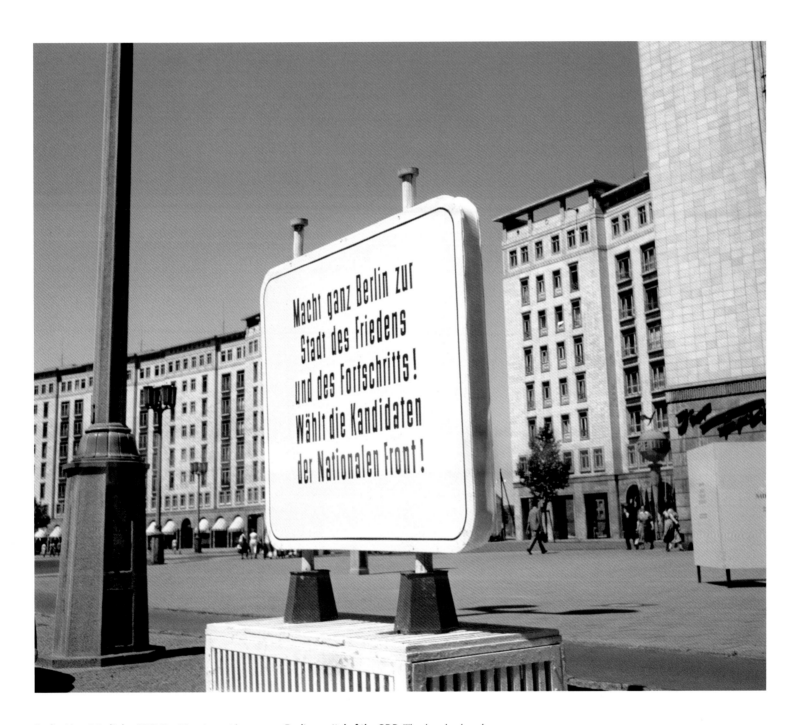

Berlin, Hauptstadt der DDR. Das Vorzeigeprojekt Stalinallee erntet im Westen nur Hohn und Spott. Ihre Architektur charakterisiert die Kritik als einen in Moskau ausgeliehenen „Zuckerbäckerstil". Aber bald schon konnte sich die DDR solche pompöse Repräsentation nicht mehr leisten. Findige Baumeister und Ingenieure entwickelten eine Bauweise aus standardisierten Einzelteilen: „die Platte". *1959*

Berlin, capital of the GDR. The show boulevard "Stalinallee" earns nothing but scorn and derision in the West. Critics describe its architecture as "wedding-cake style" borrowed from Moscow. But the GDR will soon no longer be able to afford such ostentatious prestige projects. Resourceful architects and engineers developed a method of construction using standardized individual components: the "Platte". *1959*

Links:
Die Mauer in Berlin an der Stresemannstraße, links die Ruine des Vergnügungstempels „Haus Vaterland", zwischen den Häusern ein Durchblick auf den Potsdamer Platz. *1962*

Links:
Die Mauer in Berlin an der Stresemannstraße, links die Ruine des Vergnügungstempels „Haus Vaterland", zwischen den Häusern ein Durchblick auf den Potsdamer Platz. *1962*

Left:
The Wall in Berlin on Stresemannstraße. On the left, the ruins of the pleasure dome and restaurant complex "Haus Vaterland", with Potsdamer Platz visible beyond the houses. *1962*

Unten:
Die Flucht aus dem selbst ernannten „Arbeiter- und Bauernparadies" der DDR endete oft tödlich.
Bernd Lünser, dessen an dieser Stelle in Berlin gedacht wird, hatten Volkspolizisten in den tödlichen Sprung vom Dach gehetzt. *1962*

Below:
Flight from the self-proclaimed "workers' and peasants' paradise" of the GDR often ends fatally.
Bernd Lünser, who is commemorated at this spot in Berlin, was driven by people's police to jump to his death from the roof. *1962*

Links:

Links:

„Brücke der Einheit" wird die Bösebrücke genannt.
Der metaphorische Name spielt darauf an, dass sie im
November 1989 der erste Grenzübergang war, an dem
die Grenzschranken fielen. *1962*

Left:

The Bösebrücke is popularly known as "Unity Bridge",
alluding to its role as the first border crossing that was
breached during the fall of the Berlin Wall in November
1989. *1962*

Unten:

**In zweierlei Uniformen stehen sich an der Mauer in
Berlin die Deutschen gegenüber** – ein Westberliner
Zollbeamter, zwei DDR-Grenzsoldaten. *1962*

Below:

**Germans in different uniforms confront each other
at the Wall in Berlin** – a West Berlin customs officer,
two GDR border guards. *1962*

Oben:

**Kennedys Besuch gilt dem eingemauerten West-
berlin und der US-Armee in Deutschland.** Auf der
Rhein-Main-Air Base in Frankfurt wird er mit militäri-
schem Zeremoniell begrüßt. *1963*

Above:

**Kennedy's visit is about the Wall around West Berlin
and the US army in Germany.** He is greeted with military ceremonial at the Rhine-Main Air Base in Frankfurt.
1963

Rechts:

Dienstgesichter in Frankfurt am Main: Der Präsident
blickt freundlich, die Bodyguards finster. Sie haben seinen
frühen Tod durch die Schüsse in Dallas nicht verhindern
können. *1963*

Right:

The faces of officialdom in Frankfurt/Main: the
president's expression is friendly, the bodyguards look
fierce. They were not able to prevent his untimely death
by shooting in Dallas. *1963*

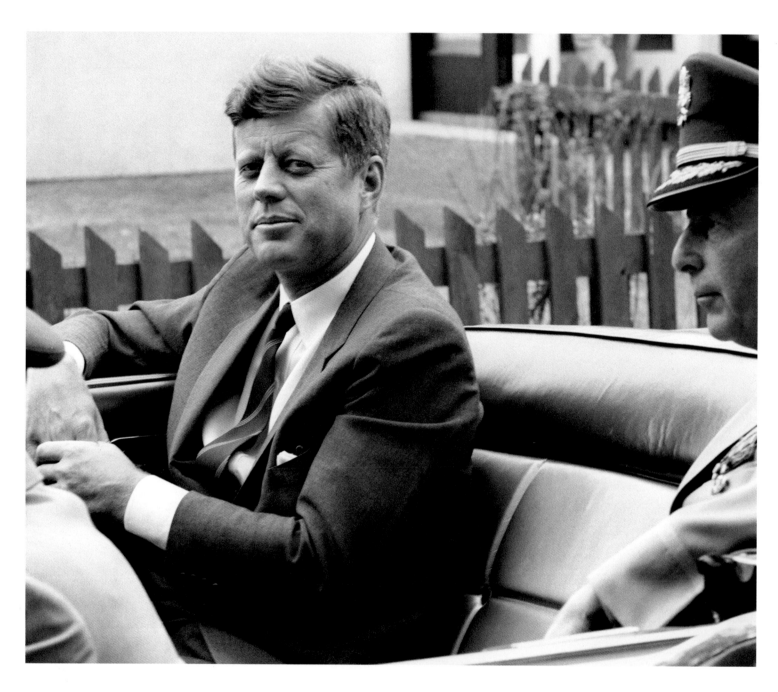

Genauso wie in Frankfurt am Main wird Präsident Kennedy im offenen Präsidentenwagen sitzen, als er wenige Monate später, am 22. November, erschossen werden sollte. Die Hintergründe bleiben rätselhaft. *1963*

Just like in Frankfurt/Main, President Kennedy will be sitting in the open presidential car when he is shot dead a few months later on 22 November. The facts remain unclear. *1963*

Schulkinder schwenken US-Fahnen in Frankfurt am Main. Eine Krankenschwester tritt aus lauter Begeisterung für den jungen amerikanischen Präsidenten vor die Absperrung der Polizei. Kennedy ist in Deutschland so beliebt wie kein US-Präsident zuvor oder danach. Seine ernsthaften Bemühungen, die frostigen Beziehungen zwischen den Machtblöcken West und Ost zu entspannen, und die humane Orientierung seiner Politik fördern seine Popularität. Nicht zuletzt sorgt sein Charisma, seine gewinnende Ausstrahlung, für Sympathie. Dank seiner Jugendlichkeit steht er für einen Umbruch in der erstarrten Nachkriegspolitik. *1963*

Schoolchildren wave American flags in Frankfurt/ Main. A nurse steps out from behind the police barrier in her enthusiasm for the young American president. Kennedy is more popular in Germany than any other US president before or since. His serious attempts to ease the frosty relations between the power blocs of West and East and the humane impulse behind his politics do a lot for his popularity. And of course his charisma, the charm he radiated, won people's hearts. With his youthful aura, he stands for a sea change in the ossified state of postwar politics. *1963*

Links:

„Spiegel"-Herausgeber Rudolf Augstein (rechts) und Finanzminister Franz Josef Strauß. Als Verteidigungsminister hatte dieser den Journalisten vier Jahre zuvor unter dem Vorwurf, Landesverrat begangen zu haben, einsperren lassen. Damit rief er die erste große politische Krise der Bundesrepublik Deutschland hervor und musste sein Amt nach starkem öffentlichen Protest quittieren. Unter dem Titel „Bedingt abwehrbereit" hatte das einflussreiche Nachrichtenmagazin „Der Spiegel" über die mangelhafte Einsatzbereitschaft der Bundeswehr berichtet. Links der Redakteur Leo Brawand. *1966*

Left:

***Spiegel* publisher Rudolf Augstein and finance minister Franz Josef Strauß.** Four years earlier, as defence minister, Strauß had accused Augstein of treason and had him sent to prison. In doing so, he provoked the Federal Republic's first serious political crisis and after vehement public protests was forced to resign. Under the title of "Partly ready for defence" the influential news magazine *Der Spiegel* had reported the inadequate operational readiness of the federal army. Editor Leo Brawand is on the left. *1966*

Unten:

Günter Grass erhebt den Zeigefinger, und alle hören zu, u.a. Ingeborg Bachmann, Willy Brandt, Karl Schiller, Hans Werner Henze, Rut Brandt, Fritz Kortner. Bei einer Veranstaltung in Bayreuth trifft Kultur auf Politik. Dank Brandt bessert sich das gestörte Verhältnis der deutschen Intellektuellen zum eigenen Land und seinem politischen System. Vielen von ihnen erschien es sklerotisch, verlogen, prüde und restaurativ. *1965*

Below:

Günter Grass wags his finger and everyone listens, a.o. Ingeborg Bachmann, Willy Brandt, Karl Schiller, Hans Werner Henze, Rut Brandt, Fritz Kortner. Culture and politics meet at a special function in Bayreuth. Thanks to Brandt, there is an improvement in the troubled relationship of German intellectuals to their country and its political system. Many of them saw it as sclerotic, hypocritical, prudish and reactionary. *1965*

Rechts:
Beim Bundespresseball. Bundeskanzler Kiesinger, FDP-Vorsitzender Scheel, Außenminister Brandt und der unaufhaltsam ins Scheinwerferlicht vorrückende CDU-Fraktionsvorsitzende Helmut Kohl amüsieren sich über einen Scherz im Ball-Almanach. *Bonn 1967*

Right:
At the federal press ball. Enjoying a joke in the almanac are Federal Chancellor Kiesinger, FDP chairman Scheel, foreign minister Brandt and CDU leader Helmut Kohl, who is moving unstoppably into the limelight. *Bonn 1967*

Oben:
Nobel. Willy Brandt im Frack und seine Frau Rut in großer Abendrobe sind ausgehbereit für den Bundespresseball in Bonn, das gesellschaftliche „Highlight" der „Bonner Republik". *1967*

Above:
Very swish. Willy Brandt in tails and his wife Rut in elegant evening dress are ready to go out to the federal press ball in Bonn, the social "highlight" of the "Bonn Republic". *1967*

Konrad Adenauer, erster Bundeskanzler der Bundesrepublik. Seine Politik einer betonten Westbindung mit den Fixpunkten Washington–Paris–Rom prägt die deutsche Politik bis 1989 und verändert das Land gesellschaftlich und kulturell von Grund auf. Im Inneren unterbleibt während seiner autoritären Kanzlerdemokratie die notwendige Schlussabrechnung mit dem Nationalsozialismus. Mit 8,5 Millionen NSDAP-Mitgliedern (Stand 1945) waren zu viele verstrickt. *1966*

Konrad Adenauer, the Federal Republic's first chancellor. His strong advocacy of integration with the West, with Washington–Paris– Rome as fixed points, determines the shape of German politics until 1989 and radically transforms the country both socially and culturally. On the domestic front, under his authoritarian "chancellor democracy", there is a failure to render the necessary final account in the matter of National Socialism. With 8.5 million members of the NSDAP (the figure in1945), too many people were involved. *1966*

Große Koalition im Park des Bundeskanzleramtes in Bonn. Das Kabinett unter Bundeskanzler Kurt Georg Kiesinger und Außenminister Willy Brandt nutzt die sommerliche Witterung, um ruhige Gelassenheit und harmonische Zusammenarbeit zu demonstrieren. Am 1. Dezember war der baden-württembergische Ministerpräsident Kiesinger in dieses Amt gewählt worden. Die Öffentlichkeit vermisst bereits nach kurzer Zeit energisches politisches Handeln und registriert Stillstand. *1967*

Grand coalition in the gardens of the Federal Chancellery in Bonn. The cabinet under Chancellor Kurt Georg Kiesinger and foreign minister Willy Brandt take advantage of the fine summer weather to demonstrate relaxed equanimity and harmonious co-operation. Baden Württemberg's prime minister Kiesinger had been elected Chancellor on 1 December. The public soon begins to feel the lack of forceful political action and registers a standstill. *1967*

MARSHALL·PLAN

Chronik der Bundesrepublik Deutschland 1945–1967

Von Gabriele Honnef-Harling

1945

30.4. Adolf Hitler begeht Selbstmord im Berliner Führerbunker.

7./8.5. Mit der Unterzeichnung der bedingungslosen deutschen Kapitulation in Reims und Berlin-Karlshorst endet der Zweite Weltkrieg in Europa.

5.6. Die vier Siegermächte übernehmen mit der Berliner Erklärung die oberste Regierungsgewalt in Deutschland. Deutschland wird in vier Besatzungszonen, die amerikanische, die britische, die französische und die sowjetische Besatzungszone, aufgeteilt, Berlin in vier Sektoren.

15.6. Gründung der Sozialdemokratischen Partei Deutschlands (SPD) in Berlin.

17.6. Gründung der Christlich-Demokratischen Union (CDU) in Köln.

17.7.–2.8. Die Siegermächte treffen sich in Potsdam. Die Konferenz der „Großen Drei" mit Harry S. Truman, Winston S. Churchill bzw. Clement R. Attlee und Josef W. Stalin regelt die künftige Politik der Alliierten für Deutschland.

20.11. In Nürnberg beginnt der Prozess gegen 24 Hauptkriegsverbrecher.

1946

21.2. In Hamburg erscheint die erste Ausgabe der politischen Wochenzeitung „Die Zeit".

26.3. Der Alliierte Kontrollrat beschränkt die Kapazitäten der gesamtdeutschen Rohstoff- und Fertigungsindustrie auf etwa die Hälfte der Vorkriegsproduktion. Der Bausektor bleibt ausgenommen.

1.10. Zwölf Angeklagte, darunter Hermann Göring, werden im Nürnberger Prozess zum Tod, sieben zu langjährigen Haftstrafen verurteilt und drei freigesprochen.

22.12. Das Saarland wird wirtschaftlich an Frankreich angegliedert.

1947

4.1. Die erste Ausgabe des Nachrichtenmagazins „Der Spiegel" erscheint.

12.3. Verkündung der „Truman-Doktrin" zur Eindämmung (Containment) des Kommunismus.

22.–25.4. Gründung des Deutschen Gewerkschaftsbundes (DGB).

5.6. US-Außenminister George C. Marshall kündigt ein Wiederaufbauprogramm für Europa und Deutschland an, den sogenannten Marshall-Plan.

29.8. Einigung der drei westlichen Besatzungsmächte auf einen neuen Industrieplan, der eine Erhöhung der Produktion auf 90 % des Standes von 1936 zulässt.

25.11.–15.12. Auf einer Außenministerkonferenz der vier Siegermächte in London wird keine Einigung in der Deutschlandfrage erreicht.

1948

23.2.–6.3. Zur Sitzung der Londoner Sechsmächtekonferenz wird die Sowjetunion nicht eingeladen. Man berät über das Schicksal der westlichen Besatzungszonen.

20.3. Die sowjetischen Vertreter verlassen den Alliierten Kontrollrat. Damit endet die gemeinsame Verwaltung Deutschlands durch die vier Siegermächte.

20.6. Währungsreform durch Einführung der DM in den westlichen Besatzungszonen. Jeder Deutsche erhält ein Startkapital von 40 DM, später noch einmal 20 DM.

24.6. Die Sowjetunion beginnt als Reaktion auf die Politik der Westmächte mit der Großblockade Westberlins, das fast elf Monate lang über eine von US-General Lucius D. Clay initiierte Luftbrücke mit Waren und Lebensmitteln versorgt werden muss.

1.8. Die erste Ausgabe der Zeitschrift „Stern" erscheint.

11.12. Die liberalen Parteien der westlichen Besatzungszonen schließen sich zur FDP zusammen. Theodor Heuss wird Parteivorsitzender.

1949

22.4. Das Ruhrstatut tritt in Kraft. Danach wird die Kohle- und Stahlproduktion des Ruhrgebietes durch die westlichen Besatzungsmächte und die Beneluxstaaten kontrolliert.

10.5. Bonn wird zur vorläufigen Bundeshauptstadt gewählt.

12.5. Die Berlinblockade wird von der Sowjetunion aufgehoben.

23.5. Das Grundgesetz für die Bundesrepublik Deutschland wird vom Parlamentarischen Rat in Bonn verkündet und tritt damit in Kraft.

14.8. Bei den Wahlen zum 1. Deutschen Bundestag liegt die Wahlbeteiligung bei 78,5 %. Die SPD erhält 29,2 % der Stimmen, die CDU 25,2 %, die CSU 5,8 %, die FDP 11,9 %, die KPD 5,7 % und die DP 4,2 %.

18.8. Die Nachrichtenagenturen der drei westdeutschen Besatzungszonen schließen sich zur Deutschen Presse-Agentur (dpa) zusammen.

12.9. Theodor Heuss (FDP) wird von der Bundesversammlung zum ersten Bundespräsidenten der BRD gewählt.

15.9. Konrad Adenauer (CDU) wird vom Bundestag mit einer Stimme Mehrheit – mit seiner eigenen – zum Bundeskanzler gewählt. Er regiert mit einer Koalition aus CDU/CSU, FDP

auch morgen in Freiheit leben

CDU

und DP. Ludwig Erhard wird Wirtschaftsminister.

7.10. Gründung der Deutschen Demokratischen Republik (DDR).

12.–14.10. Gründungskongress des Deutschen Gewerkschaftsbundes (DGB) für die gesamte Bundesrepublik in München. Erster Vorsitzender wird Hans Böckler.

19.10. Der Bundesverband der Deutschen Industrie (BDI) wird gegründet.

21.10. Bundeskanzler Adenauer betont bei seiner Regierungserklärung den Alleinvertretungsanspruch der Bundesrepublik.

1950

8.2. Die Volkskammer in der DDR billigt das Gesetz zur Bildung eines Ministeriums für Staatssicherheit (MfS).

1.5. In der Bundesrepublik entfallen die letzten Lebensmittelrationierungen.

10.6. In München schließen sich die bundesdeutschen Radiostationen zur Arbeitsgemeinschaft der Rundfunkanstalten Deutschlands (ARD) zusammen.

8.7. Die Bundesrepublik wird in den Europarat zunächst als assoziiertes Mitglied, ab dem 2.5.1951 als vollberechtigtes Mitglied aufgenommen.

25.7. Walter Ulbricht wird Generalsekretär der SED.

1951

28.9. Das Bundesverfassungsgericht nimmt in Karlsruhe seine Arbeit auf.

1.11. Die Volkskammer der DDR beschließt das Gesetz über den ersten Fünfjahresplan.

1952

26.5. In Bonn wird von den Westmächten der Vertrag über die Beziehungen zwischen der Bundesrepublik Deutschland und den drei Westmächten unterzeichnet, der die Gleichberechtigung der Bundesrepublik innerhalb der westeuropäischen Gemeinschaft vorsieht. Der Ministerrat der DDR beschließt daraufhin die Errichtung einer 5 km breiten Sperrzone entlang der Demarkationslinie zur Bundesrepublik.

14.8. Die Bundesrepublik wird Mitglied des Internationalen Währungsfonds (IWF) und der Weltbank.

1.9. Das Lastenausgleichsgesetz tritt in Kraft. Es regelt Sonderleistungen für Kriegsbeschädigte, Heimatvertriebene und Flüchtlinge.

26.12. Die erste „Tagesschau" wird von der ARD gesendet.

1953

17.6. Die Erhöhung der Arbeitsnormen führt in Ostberlin zu Protesten und Streiks, die sich auf 72 Städte und zahlreiche Ortschaften in der DDR zum Aufstand gegen das kommunistische Regime ausweiten. Die Demonstrationen werden von sowjetischen Soldaten und DDR-Volkspolizisten gewaltsam niedergeschlagen.

4.8. Der 17. Juni wird in der Bundesrepublik zum „Tag der deutschen Einheit" erklärt.

9.–20.10. Konrad Adenauer wird zum Bundeskanzler gewählt und mit der Bildung seiner zweiten Regierung beauftragt.

1954

4.7. In Bern wird die Bundesrepublik mit einem 3:2-Sieg über Ungarn Fußballweltmeister.

17.7. Theodor Heuss wird erneut zum Bundespräsidenten gewählt.

1955

5.5. Die Pariser Verträge treten in Kraft. Die Bundesrepublik wird ein souveräner Staat. Abgesehen von einigen alliierten Sonderrechten wie Truppenstationierung, Berlinstatus, Wiedervereinigungs- und Friedensvertragsfrage erlischt das Besatzungsstatut.

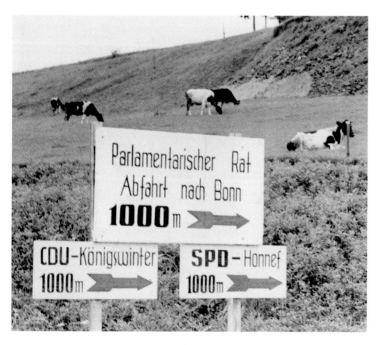

Parlamentarischer Rat
Abfahrt nach Bonn
1000 m

CDU-Königswinter
1000 m

SPD-Honnef
1000 m

In München empfingen Zehntausende jubelnder Menschen die deutsche Fußballmannschaft, die kurz zuvor in Bern im Spiel gegen die favorisierten Ungarn Weltmeister geworden war. Im offenen Mercedes v.l.n.r.: Fritz Walter, Hans Huber und der legendäre Trainer Sepp Herberger. Das Bild ist Teil eines der damals populären Sammelalben. *1954 Deutsches Historisches Museum, Berlin*

In Munich, a jubilant crowd of tens of thousands cheered the German football team on their return from securing victory in the World Cup against the favourites Hungary in Bern. In an open Mercedes from left to right: Fritz Walter, Hans Huber and the legendary coach Sepp Herberger. The picture is from one of the albums that were popular at the time. *1954 Deutsches Historisches Museum, Berlin*

9.5. Beitritt der Bundesrepublik zur NATO.

14.5. Als Gegengewicht zur NATO bilden die osteuropäischen Staaten einschließlich der DDR den Warschauer Pakt.

16.7. In Kassel wird die erste „documenta" eröffnet, die Ausstellung moderner Kunst findet von da an alle vier bis fünf Jahre statt.

8.–14.9. Bundeskanzler Adenauer reist zu einem Staatsbesuch nach Moskau. Vereinbart werden die Aufnahme diplomatischer Beziehungen und die Freilassung der letzten deutschen Kriegsgefangenen.

22.9. Bundeskanzler Adenauer verkündet vor dem Bundestag die sogenannte Hallstein-Doktrin. Danach darf die Bundesregierung – mit Ausnahme der Sowjetunion – keine diplomatischen Beziehungen mit Staaten unterhalten, die die DDR anerkennen.

23.10. Die Bevölkerung des Saarlandes lehnt in einer Volksabstimmung das Saarstatut ab, das die politische Autonomie und die wirtschaftliche Angliederung des Saarlandes an Frankreich vorsah.

12.11. Die ersten Freiwilligen der Bundeswehr erhalten vom Verteidigungsminister Theodor Blank die Ernennungsurkunden. Die Gründung der Bundeswehr ist damit vollzogen.

1956

18.1. Die Volkskammer beschließt die Schaffung der Nationalen Volksarmee.

7.7. Das Wehrpflichtgesetz wird vom Bundestag verabschiedet. Die Dauer des Wehrdienstes wird auf zwölf Monate festgelegt, ein ziviler Ersatzdienst für Kriegsdienstverweigerer eingerichtet.

27.10. Frankreich und die Bundesrepublik vereinbaren mit dem Luxemburger Vertrag die Eingliederung des Saarlandes in die Bundesrepublik Deutschland.

1957

21.1. Der Bundestag verabschiedet das Gesetz über die Rentenreform und führt damit die dynamische Rente ein. Die Renten werden nach dem Prinzip des Generationenvertrages aus den Beiträgen der aktiven Beschäftigten bezahlt.

25.3. In Rom unterzeichnen die Vertreter der Beneluxstaaten, Frankreichs, Italiens und der Bundesrepublik Deutschland die Römischen Verträge über die Gründung einer Europäischen Wirtschaftsgemeinschaft (EWG) und einer Europäischen Atomgemeinschaft (EURATOM), die am 1.1.1958 in Kraft treten.

12.4. Im „Göttinger Manifest" fordern 18 führende deutsche Atomwissenschaftler die Bundesregierung zum Verzicht auf die atomare Bewaffnung der Bundeswehr auf.

3.10. Willy Brandt wird zum Regierenden Bürgermeister von Westberlin gewählt.

22.10. Konrad Adenauer wird erneut zum Bundeskanzler gewählt, Ludwig Erhard bleibt sein Stellvertreter und Wirtschaftsminister.

1958

1.7. In der Bundesrepublik Deutschland tritt das Gesetz über die Gleichberechtigung von Mann und Frau in Kraft.

14./15.9. Das erste Treffen zwischen Bundeskanzler Adenauer und dem französischen Ministerpräsidenten de Gaulle findet in Colombey-les-Deux-Églises (Lothringen) statt.

10.11. Der sowjetische Ministerpräsident Nikita S. Chruschtschow fordert in Moskau die Aufhebung des Viermächtestatus für Berlin. Er kündigt an, dass die Sowjetunion ihren Teil der Kontrolle über Berlin an die DDR übertragen werde (Berlinkrise).

1959

1.7. Heinrich Lübke wird in Berlin zum neuen Bundespräsidenten gewählt.

13.–15.11. Auf dem Parteitag der SPD wird das „Godesberger Programm" verabschiedet. Die SPD vollzieht damit einen Wandel zur Volkspartei.

1960

8.7. Die Tarifpartner der Metallindustrie einigen sich auf die schrittweise Einführung der 40-Stunden-Woche bis 1965.

12.9. Walter Ulbricht wird Erster Staatsratsvorsitzender der DDR.

1961

11.4. In Jerusalem beginnt der Prozess gegen den ehemaligen SS-Obersturmbannführer Adolf Eichmann wegen seiner Beteiligung an der Vernichtung der Juden. Er wird zum Tod verurteilt und am 31.5.1962 hingerichtet.

6.6. Das Zweite Deutsche Fernsehen (ZDF) mit Sitz in Mainz wird als gemeinnützige Anstalt des öffentlichen Rechts gegründet.

15.6. Der DDR-Staats- und Parteichef Walter Ulbricht erklärt in einer internationalen Pressekonferenz zu Plänen für die Abriegelung der Berliner Sektorengrenze: „Niemand hat die Absicht, eine Mauer zu errichten."

13.8. Der Mauerbau beginnt. Bewaffnete Volkspolizisten der DDR fangen in der Nacht an, Ostberlin gegen Westberlin abzuriegeln.

17.9. Bei der Wahl zum 4. Deutschen Bundestag verliert die CDU/CSU die absolute Mehrheit, sie bleibt aber führende politische Kraft in der Bundesrepublik.

Nach den Jahren eines rasanten Wirtschaftswachstums setzte 1966/67 die erste ökonomische Rezession ein. Sie hatte einen Machtwechsel in Bonn zur Folge und ließ die Zeitschrift „Der Spiegel" vom 3. Januar 1966 auf dem Titelblatt besorgt fragen: „Ist das Wirtschaftswunder zu Ende?" Abgebildet ist der „Vater des Wirtschaftswunders", Bundeskanzler Ludwig Erhard. *Spiegel-Verlag, Hamburg*

After the years of rapid economic growth, in 1966/67 the first economic recession set in. It resulted in a change of government in Bonn and caused the magazine *Der Spiegel* to ask the anxious question on its title page of 3 January 1966: "Is the economic miracle over?" The cover picture is of the "Father of the economic miracle", Chancellor Ludwig Erhard. *Spiegel Verlag, Hamburg*

Unten:
Der Tod des Soziologiestudenten Benno Ohnesorg vor der Westberliner Staatsoper am 2. Juni 1967 bildet den Auftakt für die heiße Phase der Studentenrevolte. Der Protest entlädt sich in Unruhen und Straßenschlachten. In der Nacht blockieren aufgebrachte Demonstranten die Auslieferungen der Zeitungen des Springer-Verlages, denen man wegen ihrer scharfmacherischen Artikel eine Mitschuld am Tod des Studenten zumisst.
Foto: Bernard Larrson
Deutsches Historisches Museum, Berlin

Below:
The death of sociology student Benno Ohnesorg in front of the West Berlin State Opera on 2 June 1967 is the prelude to the torrid phase of the student revolution. The protest erupts in riots and street fighting. In the night, angry demonstrators blockade the distribution of newspapers from the Springer publishing house, because their rabble-rousing articles are partly blamed for the death of the student.
Photo: Bernard Larrson
Deutsches Historisches Museum, Berlin

27.10. Am Berliner Sektorengrenzübergang Checkpoint Charlie stehen sich zum ersten Mal amerikanische und sowjetische Panzer gegenüber.

7.11. Konrad Adenauer wird zum vierten Mal Bundeskanzler.

1962

26.10. Im Auftrag der Bundesanwaltschaft durchsucht die Polizei die Redaktionsräume des Nachrichtenmagazins „Der Spiegel". Der Herausgeber Rudolf Augstein und Conrad Ahlers werden unter dem Verdacht des Landesverrates verhaftet.

19.11. Die fünf FDP-Bundesminister treten zurück und fordern den Rücktritt von Verteidigungsminister Franz Josef Strauß im Zusammenhang mit der Spiegel-Affäre.

1963

22.1. Staatspräsident Charles de Gaulle und Bundeskanzler Konrad Adenauer unterzeichnen im Elysée-Palast den Vertrag über die deutsch-französische Zusammenarbeit. Der Vertrag gilt als Akt der Versöhnung beider Völker.

23.–26.6. Der amerikanische Präsident John F. Kennedy wird bei seinem Staatsbesuch in der Bundesrepublik und in Westberlin begeistert gefeiert. Seine Rede vor dem Schöneberger Rathaus beendet er mit den Worten: „Ich bin ein Berliner."

15./16.10. Bundeskanzler Adenauer tritt nach 14 Amtsjahren zurück. Sein Nachfolger wird Ludwig Erhard. Die Regierungskoalition aus CDU, CSU und FDP bleibt bestehen.

1964

1.12. Die DDR-Regierung führt für alle westlichen Besucher, abgesehen von Kindern und Rentnern, eine Mindestumtauschpflicht ein.

1965

19.9. Bei der Bundestagswahl verbessern sich CDU/CSU und SPD, die FDP erreicht nur 9,5% der abgegebenen Stimmen.

20.10. Ludwig Erhard wird zum Bundeskanzler gewählt. Sein Kabinett setzt sich wiederum aus CDU/CSU und FDP zusammen.

1966

27.10. Die Bonner Regierungskoalition wird durch einen Mehrheitsentschluss der FDP-Fraktion vorzeitig beendet.

6.11. Die NPD erreicht bei den Landtagswahlen in Hessen 7,9% der Stimmen und zieht damit erstmals in ein Landesparlament ein.

30.11. Bundeskanzler Erhard tritt nach dem Scheitern von Koalitionsverhandlungen von seinem Amt zurück.

1.12. Kurt Georg Kiesinger wird zum Bundeskanzler einer Regierung der Großen Koalition aus CDU/CSU und SPD gewählt. Der SPD-Vorsitzende Willy Brandt wird Vizekanzler und Außenminister.

1967

14.2. Unter Vorsitz von Bundeswirtschaftsminister Karl Schiller konstituiert sich in Bonn die „Konzertierte Aktion", um die Rezession besser bekämpfen zu können.

27.5.–4.6. Besuch des persischen Schahs Muhammad Reza Pahlawi und seiner Frau Farah Diba in der Bundesrepublik und in West-

berlin. Bei Demonstrationen gegen den Besuch kommt es am 2.6. in Westberlin zu Ausschreitungen. Dabei wird der 26-jährige Student Benno Ohnesorg von einem Polizisten erschossen.

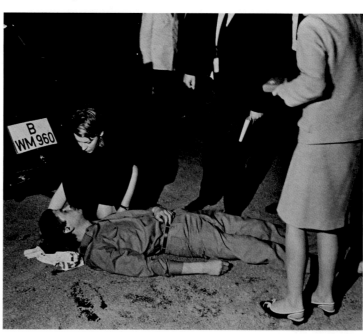

In aller Welt
zieht man den Hut

1 Million Volkswagen –

bei steigender Qualität
und sinkenden Preisen

Chronicle of the Federal Republic of Germany 1945–1967

By Gabriele Honnef-Harling

1945

30.4. Adolf Hitler commits suicide in the Führerbunker in Berlin.

7./8.5. The signing of Germany's unconditional surrender in Reims and Berlin-Karlshorst brings the Second World War to an end in Europe.

5.6. With the Berlin Declaration, the four victorious powers assume supreme authority in Germany. The country is divided into four zones of occupation – American, English, French and Soviet – and Berlin into four sectors.

15.6. Founding of the Social Democratic Party of Germany (SPD) in Berlin.

17.6. Founding of the Christian Democratic Union (CDU) in Cologne.

17.7.–2.8. The victorious powers meet in Potsdam. The conference of the "Big Three" – Harry S. Truman, Winston S. Churchill then later Clement R. Attlee and Josef W. Stalin – decides the future policies of the Allies for Germany.

20.11. The trial of 24 major war criminals begins in Nuremberg.

1946

21.2. The first edition of the political weekly newspaper *Die Zeit* appears in Hamburg.

26.3. The Allied Control Council limits the capacity of the whole of Germany's extractive and production industries to about half their pre-war levels. An exception is made for the construction industry.

1.10. In the Nuremberg trials, twelve of the accused, among them Hermann Göring, are condemned to death, seven receive long prison sentences and three are acquitted.

22.12. Saarland is annexed economically to France.

1947

4.1. The first edition of the news magazine *Der Spiegel* appears.

12.3. Proclamation of the "Truman Doctrine" for the containment of Communism.

22.–25.4. The Confederation of German Trade Unions (DGB) is set up.

5.6. US Secretary of State George C. Marshall announces a programme of reconstruction for Europe and Germany, the so-called "Marshall Plan".

29.8. The three western occupying powers agree on a new plan for industry, allowing an increase in production to 90 % of the level of 1936.

25.11.–15.12. At a conference of the foreign ministers of the four victorious powers in London there is a failure to reach agreement on the German question.

1948

23.2.–6.3. The Soviet Union is not invited to the meeting of the six-power conference in London. The topic is the fate of the western occupation zones.

20.3. The Soviet representatives leave the Allied Control Council. This means the end of the joint administration of Germany by the four victorious powers.

20.6. Monetary reform with the introduction of the Deutschmark in the western occupation zones. Every German is given a starting capital of 40 DM, later a further 20 DM.

24.6. As a response to the policies of the Western powers, the Soviet Union begins its major blockade of West Berlin. The city has to be supplied with merchandise and food for almost 11 months via an air lift organized by US General Lucius D. Clay.

1.8. The first edition of the magazine *Der Stern* appears.

11.12. The liberal parties of the western occupation zones merge to form the FDP. Theodor Heuss becomes party chairman.

1949

22.4. The Ruhr Statute comes into effect. It puts control of coal and steel production in the Ruhr into the hands of the western occupying powers and the Benelux countries.

10.5. Bonn is chosen as the provisional capital of the Federal Republic.

12.5. The Berlin blockade is lifted by the Soviet Union.

23.5. The Basic Law for the Federal Republic of Germany is proclaimed by the Parliamentary Council and thereby comes into force.

14.8. At the elections to the first German Federal Assembly, a Bundestag, the turnout is 78.5%. The SPD gets 29.2% of the votes, the CDU 25.2%, the CSU 5.8%, the FDP 11.9%, the KPD 5.7% and the DP 4.2%.

18.8. The news agencies of the three West-German occupation zones merge to form the Deutsche Presse-Agentur (dpa).

12.9. Theodor Heuss (FDP) is elected first president of the FRG by the Federal Convention.

15.9. The Bundestag elects Konrad Adenauer (CDU) federal chancellor with a majority of one vote – his own. He governs with a coalition of CDU/CSU, FDP and DP. Ludwig Erhard becomes economics minister.

7.10. Founding of the German Democratic Republic (GDR).

12.–14.10. Founding congress of the German Trade Union Federation (DGB) for Western Germany in Munich. Hans Böckler becomes its first chairman.

19.10. The Federation of German Industries (BDI) is set up.

21.10. Federal Chancellor Adenauer lays emphasis in his government policy statement on the Federal Republic's claim to sole right of representation as laid down in the Basic Law.

1950

8.2. The People's Chamber in the GDR approves the act that creates a Ministry for State Security (MfS).

1.5. End of all food rationing

10.6. In Munich the broadcasting stations in the Federal Republic merge to form the Association of German Radio Stations (ARD).

8.7. The Federal Republic is admitted to the Council of Europe, initially as an associate member, then from 2.5.1951 as a full member.

25.7. Walter Ulbricht becomes General Secretary of the SED.

1951

28.9. The Federal Constitutional Court begins its work in Karlsruhe.

1.11. The People's Chamber of the GDR enacts the law on the first Five-Year-Plan.

1952

26.5. In Bonn the three Western Allies sign the Convention on the Relations between the Three Powers and the Federal Republic of Germany, which provides for equal rights for the Federal Republic within the West-European community. In response the Council of Ministers of the GDR resolves upon the setting up of a 5-km-wide no-go area along the demarcation line with the Federal Republic.

14.8. The Federal Republic becomes a member of the International Monetary Fund and the World Bank.

1.9. The Equalization of Burdens Act comes into effect. It regulates special payments to war victims, expellees and refugees.

26.12. The first "Tagesschau" TV evening news programme is aired by the ARD.

1953

17.6. The raising of work norms leads to protests in East Berlin and strikes which spread across 72 cities and a large number of villages in the GDR in support of a revolt against the Communist regime. The demonstrations are brutally put down by Soviet soldiers and members of the GDR's People's Police.

4.8. In the Federal Republic the 17th June is declared as the "Day of German Unity".

9.–20.10. Konrad Adenauer is elected Federal Chancellor and invited to form his second government.

1954

4.7. The Federal Republic becomes Football World Champion over Hungary in Bern.

17.7. Theodor Heuss is elected federal president for a second term.

1955

5.5. The Paris Agreements come into force. The Federal Republic becomes a sovereign state. With the exception of some special privileges accorded to the Allies with regard to the stationing of troops, the status of Berlin, and reunification and peace treaty questions, the Occupation Statute is repealed.

9.5. The Federal Republic becomes a member of NATO.

14.5. As a counterbalance to NATO the countries of Eastern Europe including the GDR form the Warsaw Pact.

16.7. The first "documenta" opens in Kassel.

8.–14.9. Federal Chancellor Adenauer pays a state visit to Moscow. The establishment of diplomatic relations is agreed and the release of the last German prisoners of war.

22.9. Federal Chancellor Adenauer announces the so-called Hallstein Doctrine to the *Bundestag*. According to its provisions, the federal government may not establish or maintain diplomatic relations with any state – with the exception of the Soviet Union – that recognizes the GDR.

23.10. In a plebiscite, the people of the Saarland vote against the Saar Statute, which provided for political autonomy and economic affiliation of the Saarland with France.

12.11. The first volunteers for the Federal Armed Forces receive their certificates of appointment from Defence Minister Theodor Blank. With that, the establishment of the *Bundeswehr* is an accomplished fact.

1956

18.1. The People's Chamber votes in the formation of a National People's Army.

7.7. The Compulsory Military Service Law is passed by the Bundestag. The duration of military service is set at 12 months, and an alternative civilian service for conscientious objectors was set up.

27.10. With the Saar Treaty France and the Federal Republic agree that the Saarland should rejoin the Federal Republic of Germany.

1957

21.1. The Bundestag enacts the law on pension reform, introducing the index-linked pension. Pensions are paid from the contributions of people in active employment according to the principle of the intergenerational contract.

25.3. The representatives of the Benelux countries, France, Italy and the Federal Republic of Germany sign the Treaties of Rome dealing with the establishment of a European Economic Community (EEC) and a European Atomic Energy Community (EURATOM), which come into force on 1.1.1958.

12.4. In the "Göttingen Manifesto" 18 leading German atomic physicists call upon the federal government to forgo nuclear arms in the Bundeswehr.

3.10. Willy Brandt is elected governing mayor of West Berlin.

22.10. Konrad Adenauer is re-elected federal chancellor. Ludwig Erhard remains his deputy and economics minister.

1958

1.7. In the Federal Republic of Germany, the law establishing equal rights for men and women comes into force.

14./15.9. The first meeting between Federal Chancellor Adenauer and France's Prime Minister de Gaulle takes place in Colombey-les-Deux-Églises (Lorraine).

10.11. In Moscow, the Soviet prime minister Nikita S. Khrushchev calls for the abolition of the four-power status of Berlin. He announces that the Soviet Union is going to transfer its share of the authority over Berlin to the GDR and in so doing sparks off the so-called Berlin Crisis.

1959

1.7. Heinrich Lübke is elected the new federal president in Berlin.

13.–15.11. At the SPD party conference, the "Godesberg Programme" is ratified. With it the SPD confirms its transformation into a mainstream party.

1960

8.7. The two sides of the metal industry agree on the introduction of the 40-hour week in stages up to 1965.

12.9. Walter Ulbricht becomes the first Chairman of the Council of State.

1961

11.4. The trial begins in Jerusalem of the former SS-Obersturmbannführer Adolf Eichmann for his role in the extermination of the Jews. He is condemned to death and hanged on 31.5.1962.

6.6. The Second German Television Channel (ZDF), is established as a non-profit-making institution

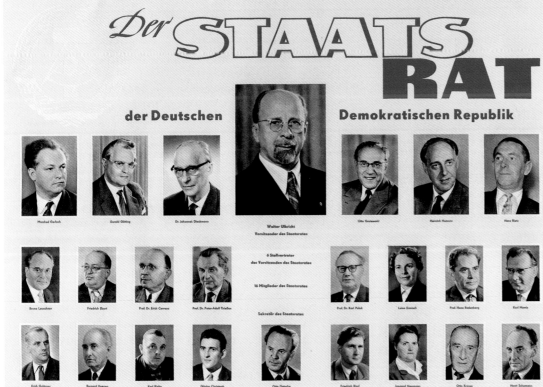

incorporated under public law with headquarters in Mainz.

15.6. The GDR's head of state and party leader Walter Ulbricht declares in an international press conference on plans to seal the sector border in Berlin: "Nobody has any intention of building a wall."

13.8. Building starts on the Wall. Armed members of the GDR's People's Police start in the night to seal East Berlin off from West Berlin.

17.9. In the elections to the fourth German Bundestag, the CDU/CSU lose the absolute majority but remain the leading political force in the Federal Republic of Germany.

27.10. At the sector crossing point Checkpoint Charlie. American and Soviet tanks face each other for the first time.

7.11. Konrad Adenauer becomes federal German chancellor for the fourth time.

1962

26.10. On the orders of the federal public prosecutor's office, the police search the offices of the news magazine *Der Spiegel*. The editor-in-chief Rudolf Augstein and Conrad Ahlers are arrested on suspicion of treason.

19.11. The five FDP ministers in the federal government resign and demand the resignation of Defence Minister Franz Josef Strauß in connection with the Spiegel affair.

1963

22.1. In the Elysée Palace, President Charles de Gaulle and Federal Chancellor Konrad Adenauer sign the Treaty on Franco-German co-operation. The treaty is seen as an act of reconciliation between the two nations.

23.–26.6. The American president John F. Kennedy is given an enthusiastic welcome on his state visit to the Federal Republic and West Berlin. He ends his speech with the words: "Ich bin ein Berliner."

15./16.10. Federal Chancellor Adenauer resigns after 14 years in office. His successor is Ludwig Erhard. The coalition of CDU, CSU and FDP remains in place.

1964

1.12. The government of the GDR introduces a mandatory minimum currency exchange for all Western visitors, with the exception of children and pensioners.

1965

19.9. In the general elections CDU/CSU and SPD improve their positions; the FDP gets only 9.5 % of the vote.

20.10. Ludwig Erhard is elected federal chancellor. His cabinet is again made up of CDU/CSU and FDP.

1966

27.10. The ruling coalition in Bonn is prematurely ended by a majority vote of the FDP parliamentary party.

6.11. The NPD gets 7.9 % of the vote in the regional elections in Hesse and is represented for the first time in a state legislature.

30.11. Federal Chancellor Erhard resigns from office after coalition negotiations fail.

1.12. Kurt Georg Kiesinger is elected federal chancellor of a government run by a grand coalition of CDU/CSU and SPD. SPD chairman Willy Brandt becomes deputy chancellor and foreign minister.

1967

14.2. Under the chairmanship of Federal Economics Minister Karl Schiller, the "Concerted Action" is set up in Bonn to make a better job of fighting the recession.

27.5.–4.6. Visit of Shah Muhammed Reza Pahlavi and his wife Farah Diba to the Federal Republic and West Berlin. Rioting breaks out during demonstrations against the visit on 2.6. in West Berlin and a 26-year-old student, Benno Ohnesorg, is shot dead by a member of the police.

ERHARD hält, was er verspricht:
Wohlstand für alle durch die
SOZIALE MARKTWIRTSCHAFT

Biografie
Buchveröffentlichungen

Josef Heinrich Darchinger

Mit Willy Brandt, Bonn. *1970 / Foto: Sven Simon*
With Willy Brandt, Bonn. *1970 / Photo: Sven Simon*

Oben rechts / Above right:
Selbstporträt im Spiegel mit AGFA Karat. *1949*
Self-portrait in mirror with Agfa Karat. *1949*

6.8.1925 Geboren in Bonn

1932–40 Volksschule

1940–42 Landwirtschaftslehre

1942 Einberufung zum Kriegsdienst

1945 Schwere Kriegsverletzung, amerikanische, später französische Kriegsgefangenschaft

1947 Nach dem dritten Versuch erfolgreiche Flucht aus der Kriegsgefangenschaft

1948 Heirat mit Ruth Hofedank, Ausbildung als Fotolaborant in der „Umkehrentwicklungsanstalt Tempo GmbH" in Bonn

1949 Kauf einer ersten Leica IIIc von einem Kriegsberichterstatter der Wehrmacht

1952 Beginn der selbstständigen Tätigkeit als Fotojournalist, zunächst vor allem für die SPD, die Friedrich-Ebert-Stiftung, Gewerkschaften, „Neuer Vorwärts" sowie andere deutsche Wochenblätter und Zeitschriften

1964 Beginn der intensiven Tätigkeit für „Der Spiegel" und „Die Zeit" mit Schwerpunkt Bundespolitik, Reisen in die westeuropäischen Länder, auch zu wichtigen internationalen Konferenzen, z.B. zur KSZE-Konferenz in Helsinki 1974, ferner in die DDR, nach Polen, in die Sowjetunion, nach China, Israel und in die arabischen Länder. Regelmäßige Zusammenarbeit mit fast allen überregionalen deutschen Zeitungen, deutschen und ausländischen Zeitschriften (z.B. „Newsweek", „L'Express", „Weltwoche"), Arbeiten für namhafte Unternehmen der Wirtschaft wie Fried. Krupp, Volkswagen, Mercedes-Benz. Für den „Spiegel" rund drei Jahrzehnte als „fester Freier" in Bonn, dabei u.a. fotografische Begleitung von über 2000 „Spiegel-Gesprächen"

1974 Bundesverdienstkreuz am Bande

1987 Dr.-Erich-Salomon-Preis der Deutschen Gesellschaft für Photographie (DGPh)

1989 Bundesverdienstkreuz 1. Klasse

1997 Große Retrospektive „Die Bonner Republik" im Rheinischen Landesmuseum, Bonn

2010 Ausstellung „Wirtschaftswunder" auf dem Fotofestival Photaumnales, Beauvais, Frankreich

2012 Ausstellung „Wirtschaftswunder – L'Allemagne après-guerre" in der Galerie Photo du Pôle Image Haute-Normandie, Rouen, Frankreich

2013 Darchinger stirbt am 28. Juli in seiner Heimatstadt Bonn

1968 Heinrich Böll. Fotografien von Chargesheimer, Jupp Darchinger und Gerd Sander. Hrsg. von Adalbert Wiemers. Bad Godesberg: Hohwacht

1974 Ulrich Blank, Jupp Darchinger: Helmut Schmidt, Bundeskanzler. Hamburg: Hoffmann und Campe

1993 Jupp Darchinger: Richard von Weizsäcker. Porträt einer Präsidentschaft. Mit Texten von Friedbert Pflüger. Düsseldorf: Econ

1993 Willy Brandt, Bilder aus dem Leben eines großen Europäers. Mit Texten von Margarita Mathiopoulos. Düsseldorf: Droemer Knaur

1996 J.H. Darchinger, Carl-Christian Kaiser: Die Köpfe. Achtzig Porträts aus der Geschichte der Republik. Mit einem Essay von Klaus Honnef. Bonn: Bouvier

1997 Die Bonner Republik. Bilder – Menschen – Ereignisse. Hrsg. von Klaus Honnef. Mit Texten von Helmut Schmidt, Klaus Honnef und Frank-Günter Zehnder. Bildlegenden von Josef H. und Frank Darchinger. Köln: Rheinland-Verlag

2004 Willy Brandt. Kämpfer und Visionär. Fotografien von Jupp Darchinger. Hrsg. von Mirja Linnekugel und Klaus Wettig. Berlin: Parthas

2008 Josef Heinrich Darchinger: Wirtschaftswunder, Deutschland nach dem Krieg 1952–1967. Hrsg. von Frank Darchinger. Mit Texten von Klaus Honnef. Köln: TASCHEN

2008 Helmut Schmidt. Fotografien von Jupp Darchinger. Hrsg. von Dieter Dowe und Michael Schneider. Bonn: Dietz

2009 Die SPD im Deutschen Bundestag. Fotografien von Jupp, Frank und Marc Darchinger. Hrsg. von Friedhelm Boll. Bonn: Dietz

Biography
Publications

Josef Heinrich Darchinger

Born 6.8.1925 in Bonn

1932–40 Elementary school

1940–42 Apprenticed as an agricultural worker

1942 Called up for military service

1945 Badly wounded in action, prisoner of war, first with the Americans, later with the French

1947 Succeeded in escaping from captivity after three attempts

1948 Married Ruth Hofedank. Trained as a photo laboratory technician in the reversal processing firm Tempo GmbH

1949 Bought his first Leica IIIc from a Wehrmacht war correspondent

1952 Began working as a freelance

Mit Josef Kardinal Ratzinger, dem späteren Papst Benedikt XVI., Rom. *1986*
With Cardinal Josef Ratzinger, later Pope Benedikt XVI., Rome. *1986*

Oben rechts / Above right:
Mit Helmut und Loki Schmidt vor dem Ferienhaus am Brahmsee. *1974*
Foto: Susanne Schmidt
With Helmut and Loki Schmidt outside their holiday home on Lake Brahmsee. *1974*
Photo: Susanne Schmidt

photojournalist, his first clients including the SPD, Friedrich-Ebert Foundation, the unions, *Neuer Vorwärts* and other German weeklies and magazines.

1964 Start of intensive work for *Der Spiegel* and *Die Zeit* with focus on federal politics. Travelled to the countries of Western Europe, also to major international conferences such as the CSCE conference in 1974 in Helsinki; also went to the GDR, Poland, the Soviet Union, China, Israel and the Arab countries. Worked on a regular basis with almost all the German national news-

papers, and with German and foreign magazines (e.g. *Newsweek, L'Express, Weltwoche*). Assignments from prestigious business enterprises like Friedrich Krupp, Volkswagen, Mercedes-Benz. Worked for around three decades as a permanent freelancer for *Der Spiegel* in Bonn, including photographing over two thousand "*Spiegel* interviews".

1974 Federal Cross of Merit on Ribbon

1987 Recipient of the Dr.-Erich-Salomon-Preis given by the German Photographic Society (DGPh)

1989 Federal Cross of Merit, First Class

1997 Major retrospective "Die Bonner Republik" at the Rheinisches Landesmuseum, Bonn

2010 Exhibition "Wirtschaftswunder" at the Photaumnales, Beauvais, France

2012 Exhibition "Wirtschaftswunder – L'Allemagne après-guerre" at the Galerie Photo du Pôle Image Haute-Normandie, Rouen, France

2013 Darchinger dies in his home town of Bonn on July 28

1968 Heinrich Böll. Photographed by Chargesheimer, Jupp Darchinger and Gerd Sander. Edited by Adalbert Wiemers. Bad Godesberg: Hohwach

1974 Ulrich Blank, Jupp Darchinger: Helmut Schmidt, Bundeskanzler. Hamburg: Hoffmann und Campe

1993 Jupp Darchinger: Richard von

Weizsäcker. Porträt einer Präsidentschaft. With texts by Friedbert Pflüger. Düsseldorf: Econ

1993 Willy Brandt, Bilder aus dem Leben eines großen Europäers. With texts by Margarita Mathiopoulos. Düsseldorf: Droemer Knaur

1996 J.H. Darchinger, Carl-Christian Kaiser: Die Köpfe. Achtzig Porträts aus der Geschichte der Republik. With an essay by Klaus Honnef. Bonn: Bouvier

1997 Die Bonner Republik. Bilder – Menschen – Ereignisse. Edited by Klaus Honnef. With texts by Helmut Schmidt, Klaus Honnef and Frank-Günter Zehnder. Captions by Josef H. and Frank Darchinger. Cologne: Rheinland

2004 Willy Brandt. Kämpfer und Visionär. Photographed by Jupp Darchinger. Edited by Mirja Linnekugel and Klaus Wettig. Berlin: Parthas

2008 Josef Heinrich Darchinger: Wirtschaftswunder, Germany after the war 1952–1967. Edited by Frank Darchinger. With texts by Klaus Honnef. Cologne: TASCHEN

2008 Helmut Schmidt. Photographed by Jupp Darchinger. Edited by Dieter Dowe and Michael Schneider. Bonn: Dietz

2009 Die SPD im Deutschen Bundestag. Photographed by Jupp, Frank and Marc Darchinger. Edited by Friedhelm Boll. Bonn: Dietz

Index

Impressum/Imprint

EACH AND EVERY TASCHEN BOOK PLANTS A SEED!
TASCHEN is a carbon neutral publisher. Each year, we offset our annual carbon emissions with carbon credits at the Instituto Terra, a reforestation program in Minas Gerais, Brazil, founded by Lélia and Sebastião Salgado. To find out more about this ecological partnership, please check: *www.taschen.com/zerocarbon*
Inspiration: unlimited.
Carbon footprint: zero.

To stay informed about TASCHEN and our upcoming titles, please subscribe to our free magazine at *www.taschen.com/magazine*, follow us on Twitter, Instagram, and Facebook, or e-mail your questions to *contact@taschen.com*.

© 2017 TASCHEN GmbH
Hohenzollernring 53
D-50672 Cologne
www.taschen.com

Original edition:
© 2008 TASCHEN GmbH

© 2008 Josef Heinrich Darchinger, Bonn, Friedrich-Ebert-Stiftung, Bonn
© 2008 Klaus Honnef, Bonn

Printed in China
ISBN 978–3–8365–4016–2

Captions:
Frank Darchinger, Klaus Honnef and Gabriele Honnef-Harling, Bonn

Chronology:
Gabriele Honnef-Harling, Bonn

Editorial coordination:
Simone Philippi, Cologne
Jascha Kempe, Cologne

Design:
Sense/Net Art Direction,
Andy Disl and Birgit Eichwede, Cologne,
www.sense-net.net

Final Artwork:
Tanja da Silva, Cologne

Production coordination:
Stefan Klatte, Cologne

English translation:
Hilary Heltay, Hereford

Seite 2:
Kinder auf einem Trümmergrundstück in Köln. Die weniger zerstörten Teile des Hauses sind bewohnt. *1956*

Page 2:
Children on a bomb site in Cologne. There are still people living in the less damaged parts of the house. *1956*

Seite 4:
Die Innenstädte erstrahlen im hellen Licht der Kaufhäuser wie Neckermann in Frankfurt. Knapp zwanzig Jahre nach dem verlorenen Krieg demonstrieren die erleuchteten Fassaden stolz den erreichten Wohlstand. Im Vordergrund eine Mercedes-Benz-Limousine Typ 220, das neue Statussymbol. Der Versandhauskönig und spätere Reiseunternehmer Josef Neckermann ist eine Symbolfigur des „Wiederaufbaus". Sein Slogan „Neckermann macht's möglich" ist die Fanfare eines bis dato ungekannten Massenwohlstandes. Ende der 1960er Jahre schlug der Versandhandel fast 5 % des gesamten Einzelhandelsvolumens um. *1964*

Page 4:
The city centres are all aglow with the bright lights of department stores like Neckermann in Frankfurt. Not quite twenty years after the lost war, the illuminated façades proudly proclaim the affluence that has been achieved. In the foreground a Mercedes-Benz 220 Saloon, the new status symbol. The mail-order magnate and later tour operator Josef Neckermann is an icon of the "reconstruction". His slogan "Neckermann makes it possible" is the fanfare of a hitherto unknown mass prosperity. At the end of the Sixties, the mail-order business accounted for almost 5% of the total volume of the retail trade. *1964*